THE ART OF THE
PRE-RAPHAELITES

THE ART OF THE
PRE-RAPHAELITES

STEVEN ADAMS

CHARTWELL
BOOKS INC.

A QUINTET BOOK

Published by Chartwell Books
A Division of Book Sales, Inc.
110 Enterprise Avenue
Secaucus, New Jersey 07094

Reprinted 1994

ISBN 0-7858-0199-5

This book was designed and produced by
Quintet Publishing Limited
6 Blundell Street
London N7 9BH

Creative Director: Peter Bridgewater
Art Director: Ian Hunt
Designer: Nicki Simmonds
Editors: Patricia Bayer, Judith Simons
Picture Researcher: Joseline Toresse

Typeset in Great Britain by
Central Southern Typesetters, Eastbourne
Manufactured in Hong Kong by
Regent Publishing Services Limited
Printed in China

PICTURE CREDITS

Key: l = left; r = right; t = top; b = bottom.

Page 6 Birmingham Museum and Art Gallery (Photo Bridgeman Art Library); **7 l** Tate Gallery, London (Photo Bridgeman Art Library); **7 r** Uffizi Gallery, Florence (Photo Bridgeman Art Library); **8 l** Tate Gallery, London (Photo Bridgeman Art Library); **8/9** Walker Art Gallery, Liverpool, National Museums and Galleries on Merseyside; **10** Tate Gallery, London (Photo ET Archive); **11** Victoria & Albert Museum, London (Photo Bridgeman Art Library); **12** Kunstmuseum, Dusseldorf (Photo Fabbri/Bridgeman); **14** Stanza della Segnatura, Vatican (Photo ET Archive/Dagli Orti); **15** Tate Gallery, London (Photo ET Archive); **16** Walker Art Gallery, Liverpool, National Museums and Galleries on Merseyside; **17** Huntington Library (Photo Visual Arts Library); **18** Staatliche Museum, Berlin (Photo Visual Arts Library); **19** Staatliche Kunstsammlungen, Dresden (Photo Bridgeman Art Library); **20** National Gallery, Berlin (Photo Visual Arts Library); **21** Louvre, Paris (Photo Bridgeman Art Library); **22 t b** Staatliche Museum, Berlin (Photo Fabbri/Bridgeman); **25** Ludwigskirche, Monaco (Photo Fabbri/Bridgeman); **26** Birmingham City Art Gallery (Photo Bridgeman Art Library); **28/9** Johannesburg Art Gallery (Photo Bridgeman Art Library); **30** Bradford City Art Gallery and Museums (Photo Bridgeman Art Library); **31** Walker Art Gallery, Liverpool, National Museums and Galleries on Merseyside; **32/3** Tate Gallery, London (Photo ET Archive); **34** Tate Gallery, London (Photo ET Archive); **37** Ashmolean Museum, Oxford, **39** Keble College, Oxford (Photo Bridgeman Art Library); **40** Uffizi Gallery, London (Photo Bridgeman Art Library); **42** Victoria & Albert Museum, London (Photo Bridgeman Art Library); **43** The Ruskin Gallery, Sheffield; **44/5** Kenwood House, London (Photo ET Archive); **46** Cleveland Museum of Art (Photo Visual Arts Library); **47** Tate Gallery, London (Photo ET Archive); **48/9** Fitzwilliam Museum, Cambridge (Photo Visual Arts Library); **50** Museo San Marco, Florence (Photo Giraudon/Bridgeman); **51** Gemalde Galerie, Berlin (Photo Visual Arts Library); **52** Private Collection (Photo Bridgeman Art Library); **53, 54/5, 56** The Ruskin Gallery, Sheffield (The Guild of St George Collection); **58** Private Collection (Photo Bridgeman Art Library); **60** Photo Visual Arts Library; **61** Lady Lever Art Gallery, Merseyside (Photo Bridgeman Art Library); **62** Royal Academy, London (Photo Visual Arts Library); **63** Tate Gallery, London (Photo ET Archive); **64** Private Collection (Photo ET Archive); **65** Visual Arts Library; **66 l** National Portrait Gallery, London (Photo ET Archive); **66 r** Victoria & Albert Museum, London (Photo Bridgeman Art Library); **67 l r** Photo P D Cormack; **68, 69 l r** William Morris Gallery, London (Photo Visual Arts Library); **70, 71** Tate Gallery, London (Photo Bridgeman Art Library); **72/73** Christie's, London (Photo Bridgeman Art Library); **75** Birmingham City Art Gallery (Photo Bridgeman Art Library); **76** Manchester Art Gallery (Photo Visual Arts Library); **77** Walker Art Gallery, Liverpool, National Museums and Galleries on Merseyside; **78** The Brooklyn Museum, New York; **81** Cincinnati Art Museum (Photo Visual Arts Library); **82/3** Photo Visual Arts Library; **84** Manchester Art Gallery (Photo Visual Arts Library); **86/7** Tate Gallery, London (Photo ET Archive); **90** The Pierpont Morgan Library, New York; **91** Private Collection; **92** Metropolitan Museum of Art, New York; **93** Collection of Mr & Mrs Wilbur L Ross Jr, New York; **94** New York Historical Society; **95** Photo Visual Arts Library; **96** Metropolitan Museum of Art, New York; **97** The Brooklyn Museum; **98** Guildhall Art Gallery, London (Photo Bridgeman Art Library); **100** Private Collection (Photo Bridgeman Art Library); **101** San Rocco, Venice (Photo Visual Arts Library); **102** Tate Gallery, London (Photo Bridgeman Art Library); **103** Tate Gallery, London (Photo ET Archive); **105** Private Collection (Photo Bridgeman Art Library); **106** Detroit Institute of Arts (Photo Bridgeman Art Library); **108** Manchester City Art Gallery (Photo Bridgeman Art Library); **109** Lady Lever Art Gallery, National Museums and Galleries on Merseyside; **110** Tate Gallery, London (Photo Bridgeman Art Library); **111** Musée d'Orsay, Paris (Photo Lauros-Giraudon/Bridgeman); **112/3** Roy Miles Fine Paintings, London (Photo Bridgeman Art Library); **114** Manchester City Art Gallery (Photo Bridgeman Art Library); **115** Lady Lever Art Gallery, National Museums and Galleries on Merseyside (Photo Visual Arts Library); **116** Manchester City Art Gallery (Photo Bridgeman Art Library); **117** Birmingham City Art Gallery (Photo Bridgeman Art Library); **118** Lady Lever Art Gallery, National Museums and Galleries on Merseyside (Photo Bridgeman Art Library); **119** Guildhall Art Gallery, London (Photo Bridgeman Art Library); **121, 122** Elida Gibbs Collection, London (Photo Bridgeman Art Library).

CONTENTS

INTRODUCTION

Ford Madox Brown, The Last of
England, *1852–5. The painting, on
the theme of middle-class emigration,
was inspired by Thomas Woolner's
own departure for Australia in July
1852.*

The Pre-Raphaelite Brotherhood was founded in London in the autumn of 1848, adopting its name in deference to painters working before the time of Raphael. This secret society had been convened by Dante Gabriel Rossetti, William Holman Hunt and John Everett Millais, and was extended to include two more painters, James Collinson and FG Stephens; a sculptor, Thomas Woolner, and the tax clerk, William Michael Rossetti, brother of Dante Gabriel and diarist and secretary to the Pre-Raphaelite circle.

The aim of the seven was an ambitious one: to reform the standards of English painting, which in the Victorian era had sunk to a lamentably mediocre level. Enshrined within the Royal Academy, a bastion of conservative artistic taste, was a style and method of painting originally invented in 16th-century Italy and still being applied centuries later in some quarters. In the hands of Raphael and his successors this refined style, which was to become the cornerstone of academic teaching throughout Europe and beyond,

....
Dante Gabriel Rossetti, The
Girlhood of Mary Virgin, *1848–
49. Rossetti's image of the adolescent
Virgin Mary was the first of his
pictures to carry the impress PRB.*
....

....
Fra Angelico, The Coronation of
the Virgin. *The work of this 15th-
century painter, considered 'primitive'
by many Victorian connoisseurs, was
widely admired by the Pre-Raphaelite circle.*
....

had produced some of the most breathtakingly beautiful and articulate work of the High Renaissance.
However, in the hands of British artists active in the
first decade of Victoria's reign, the same academic
tradition had produced a corpus of dull and often
embarrassing pictures. It was in the context of this
lacklustre milieu that the Pre-Raphaelite Brotherhood challenged not only the Victorian artistic establishment and the entire weight of academic tradition,
but also the example of the 'Divine' Raphael himself.

The Pre-Raphaelite convenant required that, far
from following the example of a Renaissance rubric
epitomized by the work of Raphael and a pantheon of
Old Masters, painting should return to the pious,
naturalistic and unaffected approach found in the
work of artists active in the 14th and 15th centuries
— and, even more importantly, turn to Nature itself.
In 1848–49, often with more zeal than ability, the
Brotherhood produced a handful of brightly coloured

and minutely detailed pictures, depicting unconventional subjects culled from the Bible or medieval
poetry and imitating both the style and form of 14th-
and 15th-century art. Each picture bore the secret
mark of pictorial reform – the initials 'PRB'.

The aims of the Pre-Raphaelites, despite the eager-
ness with which the brethren sought to reform English art, were hardly new, and close scrutiny shows
that the immature artists were ill-aware of the intellectual position they occupied on the European cultural
stage. Even a cursory survey of those painters, poets,
architects and philosophers disaffected with the academic and rationalist traditions of the Enlightenment
would have revealed an impressive line-up of kindred
spirits stretching back at least a century. Save for a
few unfashionable enthusiasms, among them Blake,
Hogarth and Keats, the Pre-Raphaelite Brotherhood
was, at its inception, generally unaware that its programme of reform placed its members in exceptionally

....
A B O V E Henry Wallis, The Death
of Chatterton, 1856. *One of a
series of literary themes undertaken by
the artist.*
....
R I G H T Dante Gabriel Rossetti,
Dante's Dream, 1856. *The subject,
taken from the* Vita Nuova, *depicts
the author's dream of Beatrice's
death.*
....

good company – for many others had also taken flight
from the sophistication of the present to find comfort
in the primitive traditions of the distant past. In fact,
Pre-Raphaelitism's inability to see itself as part of a
wider pattern of dissent creates something of a head-
ache for the art historian. Except for some broad and
generalizing principles – an antipathy for academic
dogma, an admiration for early Italian painting hitherto dismissed by many connoissseurs, and the belief
that, painters should have 'no master except their
own powers of mind and hand, and their own first-
hand study of Nature' – the aims of the Pre-
Raphaelite Brotherhood were often vague, ill-articu-
lated and inconsistent, and consequently are difficult
to define.

The lack of some common purpose soon becomes
evident in the work of the Brotherhood. While there
is some consensus among the first pictures to carry
the PRB impress, after less than four or five years
individual brethren had begun to part company. The
often ungainly naturalism, vivid, sunlit colouring and
interest in unconventional subject matter which had
bound the Brotherhood in 1848 endured only in the
work of one member, William Holman Hunt. In others
it rapidly dissipated. Moreover, what little sense of
common purpose the artists had was eclipsed by the
powerful personality of John Ruskin. Ruskin had

Dante Gabriel Rossetti, The
Beloved, 1865–66.

found echoes of his own opinions in the works of the Brotherhood and, after an initial series of bitter attacks on their paintings, published a spirited defence of Pre-Raphaelitism in *The Times*. Ruskin emerged as the most articulate spokesman for the movement by far, and was later to attempt to play the role of theoretical incubus to several of its members, exercising — albeit only momentarily – a visible influence on the work of Millais, Rossetti and Burne-Jones.

The homogeneity of the Pre-Raphaelites was further called into question when Ruskin's book,

Modern Painters, was exported to the United States. There Ruskin's evangelical demand for a truthful rendition of nature, in preference to academic tradition, struck a resonant chord. American painters and critics, often weaned on the same Low Church sentiment as Ruskin himself, were summoned, through the medium of *Modern Painters*, to bear witness to Divine Creation itself, and in so doing they simultaneously crafted a national cultural identity and distinguished themselves from the overbearing influence of Europe.

Sir Edward Coley Burne-Jones, The
Mill, *1870.*

The notion of a Pre-Raphaelite 'movement', then, compared to the movements that dominate 20th-century art, is something of a fiction. Both the first and second generation of Pre-Raphaelites and fellow travellers in Continental Europe and the United States had jumped aboard a naturalistic bandwagon for a variety of different reasons – and few of its occupants would have agreed upon its destination. Pre-Raphaelitism in all its forms can only be understood in terms of the wider, more consistent, and more articulate artistic and intellectual climate of the period – the thesis that has determined the form of this study.

The first chapter of this book examines the academic tradition against which the Brotherhood recoiled and lends some insight into the interests of earlier painters and and writers who laid the intellectual foundations for the formation of the Pre-Raphaelite circle. The second chapter charts the inception of the Brotherhood and surveys the first Pre-Raphaelite works, perhaps the most exciting and consistent of all Pre-Raphaelite paintings. Thereafter, there is a strong case for arguing that the Pre-Raphaelite movement had virtually run its course; Millais, in fact, made precisely this contention. But by the mid-1850s there were a number of seminal works of the Pre-Raphaelite corpus still unmade; Rossetti had yet to produce some of his most lyrical studies of ideal Pre-Raphaelite womanhood and go on to inspire a second generation of artists and designers, among them William Morris and Edward Burne-Jones. The book's remaining chapters deal with these later works of Rossetti, as well as those of the original Brotherhood and the second wave of sympathetic artists, including Burne-Jones; also explored are the significant place of Ruskin and his writings in the Pre-Raphaelite sphere and manifestations of Pre-Raphaelitism in the United States.

It is important to recognize that the cause later taken up by Rossetti, who in the popular imagination became inextricably connected with the movement, was quite different in spirit to the ideals that originally had animated the Brotherhood in 1848. Hunt, the only member of the circle to observe the first articles of this faith, indeed almost to the letter, made exactly this point in his memoirs. One only has to consider the hard-headed socialism of Morris and the wistful Aestheticism of Burne-Jones to appreciate the extent to which the direction of the movement was to change further in the very latter part of the century.

In 1856 Christina Rossetti, Dante Gabriel's sister, penned a few lines of satirical verse in which she referred to the scattering of original members of the Pre-Raphaelite Brotherhood and their vastly disparate interests. Her poem, had she written it half a century later, might well have assumed epic proportions, for the process was to continue until Pre-Raphaelitism all but disappeared under the various mantles of other late 19th- and early 20th-century movements. This book attempts, in prose rather than poetry, to chart precisely that course.

CHAPTER ONE

THE

FEAST OF REASON

Peter von Cornelius, The Wise and
Foolish Virgins.

*I*n the first half of the 19th century the overwhelming authority of academic tradition – a tradition dating back to the Renaissance in Italy – began to be the subject of ridicule and censure in some circles. William Blake had annotated Sir Joshua Reynolds, 'Discourses' – the backbone of academic theory in 18th-century England – with a stream of libellous invective. Reynolds was the subject of further criticism in the third volume of John Ruskin's *Modern Painters*, and was dubbed 'Sir Sloshua' by the Pre-Raphaelite Brotherhood for his flashy technique. Both Ruskin and the Pre-Raphaelite painter FG Stephens even extended their criticism to Raphael, who was understood to embody the pinnacle of artistic achievement, in that his example was still upheld in academic circles well over three centuries after his death.

Academic teaching had not only been compromised in England. In France a group of painters known as *les primitifs* had seceded from the studio of the painter Jacques-Louis David. Their astringent tastes prompted the rejection not only of the Renaissance but also of Classical antiquity itself, to the extent that only a handful of suitably primitive authorities remained after their cultural purge; among them were the Old Testament, Homer and the works of the Nordic bard Ossian. Secessions had also occurred at academies in Vienna and Munich. Peter von Cornelius and Johann Friedrich Overbeck had left Vienna in 1803 to establish a fraternity of painters in the abandoned monastery of Sant'Isidoro in Rome. Their aim had been to emulate not only the simple and naturalistic style of medieval art but also to revive the basic Christian piety that had inspired Italian painting of the 14th and 15th centuries. In each instance the weight of academic tradition based upon the Old Masters and underwritten by antiquity had been

overturned in favour of a much less dogmatic alternative. The Pre-Raphaelite movement in Great Britain and kindred movements throughout Europe emerged to some extent as a reaction to the teachings of the academies. Their achievements can be placed in the proper context by providing some insight into the evolution of mid-19th-century academies of art and the various European movements that rose to oppose them.

The idea of an academy, a school devoted to scientific, literary and philosophical speculation, was revived in Italy by Cosimo de' Medici during the latter part of the 15th century and based upon a model founded by Plato in Athens during the 4th century BC. The first academy of painting and sculpture, however, emerged during the 16th century and sought to raise the disciplines from the realm of a humble craft practised by artisans to an intellectually respectable art that could legitimately rub shoulders with philosophical and literary interests. Leon Battista Alberti (1407–72) was one of the first Renaissance scholars to articulate the notion that painting and sculpture were not crafts but activities undertaken with the brain rather than with the hand. Alberti's ideas were of utmost importance and subsequently became a cornerstone of academic teaching. Following the example of Classical authorities such as Aristotle and Horace, Alberti stated in his treatise, *Della Pittura*, written in the middle of the century, that the purpose of painting, like that of poetry, its sister art, was to represent human nature. It was essential, however, for both the painter and the poet to refine the actions of human beings, to generalize and improve upon nature rather than to depict it exactly as it appeared. The ideal sought by painters and poets, Alberti maintained, was contained not in one exclusive object or person but dispersed in several.

In the third book of *Della Pittura*, Alberti related the story of the ancient Greek painter Zeuxis, who, commissioned to paint a portrait of the sublimely beautiful Helen of Troy, chose not one model but five, taking the best parts from each to form an ideal image that surpassed natural appearance. The tale, which was almost certainly apocryphal, had a strong appeal to artists and writers of the Renaissance and was recounted time and again throughout the 16th and 17th centuries. In his famous letter written in 1516 to Baldassare Castiglione, Raphael made precisely the same point. In order to achieve a model of feminine beauty, he stated, he must first see many

A B O V E *Sir Joshua Reynolds*, Portrait of Mrs Siddons as the Tragic Muse.

L E F T *Anton Raffael Mengs*, Self-Portrait.

beautiful women. Raphael outlined a creative process that was highly cerebral and light years away from the manual craftsmanship practised by his predecessors and advocated by the Pre-Raphaelites. Subjects for painting, the academic canon decreed, were not to be found in everyday life but were formed within the painter's own mind.

Painting, in addition to its literary connections, also gained respectability through its association with other learned pursuits, notably a corpus of secular learning that included the liberal arts of arithmetic, geometry and rhetoric. In the first book of *Della Pittura*, Alberti painstakingly described the manner in which an artist was able to give an impression of depth and space in his work – not through the study of the outside world but through the mathematical calculations of the dis-

Franz Pforr, **Knights before a Charcoal Burner's Hut.**

tortions and diminutions of objects as they receded into the distance. Some understanding of the liberal art of rhetoric was also useful to the artist. The proper subject of art was human actions. Painting was considered 'mute poetry' and it was therefore essential to ensure that the gestures and expressions of the human subjects would tell a story with eloquence. Leonardo da Vinci had, in fact, advised painters to learn this mute form of communication from the gestures made by the dumb. At the end of the Renaissance, then, painting had transcended the humble realms of the crafts with which it had traditionally been connected and could now claim to be an art practised by intellectuals and gentlemen.

The precepts outlined in the works of Alberti and Leonardo were developed by subsequent generations and emerged as a rigid and at times almost scientific doctrine. The 17th-century French preoccupation with rationalism – the idea that every phenomenon was explicable and conformed to general scientific laws – was applied to all areas of culture and enquiry.

At the Academy of painting and sculpture in Paris, Charles Le Brun (1619–90), its director, wrote a lengthy treatise on painting in which a whole array of human feelings was reduced to a supposedly rational pattern-book, or code of gestures and expressions, wherein astonishment, fear, horror and numerous other emotions were portrayed as a series of melodramatic postures. His contemporary, Roland Fréart de Chambray, had adapted Leonardo's treatise and reduced the art of painting to a series of 365 rules, in the firm belief that the secret of a good picture lay in the dogged pursuit of rules.

The authority of Classical antiquity increased as academic ideals, broadly similar to those enshrined at the *Académie Française* in Paris, spread throughout Europe. Art historian Nikolaus Pevsner identified 19

....
Caspar David Friedrich, The Cross
in the Mountains, *1808*.
....

Caspar David Friedrich, Oak in the Snow, *1829.*

Less scholarly but no less influential studies were written by the art historian Johann Joachim Winckelmann (1717–68) and the painter Anton Raffael Mengs (1728–79). Winckelmann wrote 'Thoughts on the Imitation of Greek Works . . .' in Dresden in 1755 — never having seen an original example of his subject. His enthusiasm for Greek art was nonetheless unbounded. Classical Greece, Winckelmann maintained, had not only established a timeless standard of ideal beauty in painting and sculpture but had founded the ideal on the physical reality of its own race. 'The most beautiful body of ours,' he stated, 'would perhaps be as much inferior to the most beautiful Greek one . . .'

Winckelmann had a profound influence on both the theories and the practice of his compatriot and friend Mengs, who, not surprisingly, again viewed antiquity – together with the trinity of Raphael, Correggio and Titian – as providing a timeless artistic standard. It was primarily in the example of antiquity, he maintained, that nature (refined by a 'philosophical intellect') might best be perceived. The examples of Winckelmann and Mengs were especially important in disseminating academic opinion throughout the remainder of Europe. Mengs played an active part in academies in Rome, Naples and Dresden and exerted an influence on the curricula for similar bodies in Vienna and Denmark. He was in addition responsible for writing the creed adopted by the Madrid Academy and became the principal of the Accademia in Rome. Friends, pupils and devotees also played a significant role in the process and were active in Vienna, Zurich, Leipzig and Turin.

Academic theories evolved in England in a less systematic fashion. The idea of establishing an academy of painting and sculpture under the patronage of the Crown had first been mooted in Britain early in the 18th century by the painter Sir James Thornhill. Thornhill's plan – which had been inspired by the example of the *Académie Royale* in Paris – had failed to materialize. A properly constituted academy with support from the Crown did not emerge until the end of 1768, some 40 years after Thornhill's experiment, when 40 founder-members of the new institution were appointed by George III, with Sir Joshua Reynolds (1723–92) serving as president. The aim of the new Royal Academy was to provide a repository for the great examples of painting and sculpture in order that the native genius of British painters might be 'tamed' by the example of great art. The Academy's party line was more explicitly stated by its president in

academies in Europe by 1720 and well over a hundred by the end of the 18th century. Moreover, the influence of the Classical tradition, which had remained strong since the Renaissance, grew as antiquarians began to take a more scholarly interest in the ancient world. Excavations at Herculaneum and Pompeii began in 1738 and 1748, respectively, and greatly increased understanding of the Classical past, which had hitherto remained somewhat fanciful and open to wide interpretation. An appreciation of Greek antiquity also increased during the 18th century with the publication of a number of scholarly works, including the *Recueil des Antiquités* by the Comte de Caylus; *Les Ruines de la Grèce* by Le Roi, and *Antiquities of Athens* by James Stuart and Nicholas Revett.

....
Théodore Géricault, Study for The
Raft of Medusa. *The final work
depicting the survivors of the wreck of
the Medusa was painted in 1819.*
....

the form of a series of ex-cathedra lectures, or 'Discourses', given to members, in which antiquity and the examples of Old Masters and the ancients consistently featured.

At shop-floor level, instruction came from Academicians teaching one of a variety of subjects that made up the traditional academic curriculum. Perspective, anatomy, painting, sculpture and architecture were taught and, following the principle that the highest genre in art is the interpretation of historical and literary subjects, Oliver Goldsmith and Thomas Boswell were co-opted to advise on subject matter. An example of the academic word made flesh is Reynolds' portrait of Sarah Siddons exhibited at the Royal Academy in 1784; it depicts the celebrated actress as the Muse of Tragedy, flanked by the twin genii of Pity and Terror. The theme, inspired by Classical tragedy, is suitably ennobling and consistent with Reynolds' stricture that painting should evoke some grand sentiment. The composition follows another academic principle: the pose is taken not directly from nature but is based upon Michelangelo's figure of the prophet Isaiah in the Sistine Chapel in Rome.

During the first part of the 19th century the Royal Academy began to accommodate not only paintings in the tried and tested Classical style but also pictures laden with a heavy sentimentalism. The change had been prompted by the gradual demise of the Whig faction in British social life and the rise of self-made, middle-class men and women. The middle classes had not, on the whole, had access to a Classical education and consequently replaced Greek and Roman mythology with sentimental scenes of everyday life focusing upon such themes as the home, motherhood, the virtues of labour and so on. John Ruskin commented on

Peter von Cornelius,
Joseph Recognised by
his Brothers.

Friedrich Johann Overbeck,
Joseph Being Sold by
his Brothers, *1816.*

the anodyne standards of academic art by comparing the Royal Academy with the famous London grocery store of Fortnum & Mason, both of which, in their respective fields, moderated 'the mild tastes' of the British public.

The refined tastes that had developed throughout Europe in the wake of hackneyed academicism had been the subject of continual attacks from a variety of factions, and it was in this general climate of revolt that the Pre-Raphaelite Brotherhood emerged. The revolt against academicism predated the foundation of the Pre-Raphaelites by some 50 years and took on various forms. In 19th-century Germany, the *Sturm und Drang* ('Storm and Stress') movement emphasized the importance of individual inspiration and self-expression in painting. Its exponents maintained that the fundamentals of art could not be taught, as the academies upheld, because artistic merit was resident in the artist's imagination rather than in some academic textbook. The career of the Romantic painter, Philipp Otto Runge (1777–1810), demonstrates this strong antipathy toward academic training. In 1801 he abandoned an academic training in Copenhagen and went to Dresden, where he resorted to a realistic style of landscape painting heavily infused with a personal symbolism. A similar symbolism is found in the paintings of Caspar David Friedrich (1774–1840). His pictures, like those of Runge, evince a preoccupation with romantic imagery. Human figures, trees, ships or crosses stand in lonely Ossianic landscapes, inspired, in many instances, by the poetry of Ludwig Tieck and the Schlegel brothers.

Romanticism in France took on a quite different but equally dissident form. Painters such as Théodore Géricault (1791–1824) drew from a repertoire of awesome and often violent images. His monumental celebrated painting of the *Raft of the Medusa,* completed in 1819, commemorates a contemporary event in which 149 people were cut adrift on a lifeboat after having been shipwrecked off the coast of Senegal. The occupants were sustained only by cannibalism and the incident became a national scandal. No less violent were the Shakespearean tragedies which, having been largely ignored for centuries, began to enjoy a vogue in early 19th-century Paris. French theatre had been dominated by precisely the same preoccupation with rules that had beset painting since the foundation of the *Académie Française* in 1634. Shakespeare rode roughshod over many of those rules and became something of a Romantic hero for both painters and

writers. Stendhal had celebrated his influence in an 1824 essay, 'Racine et Shakespeare', in which the Bard's example was upheld in preference to French classicism. Further instances can be cited wherein painters (and writers) active in the first half of the 19th century began to appreciate the limitations of academic doctrine and thus apply themselves to other solutions. One alternative to the Classical creed which had a profound influence on the Pre-Raphaelite movement was an interest in early Christian art.

European academies consistently had been distracted by the examples of Classical and Renaissance cultures, to the extent that medieval painting had often been dismissed as merely 'primitive'. Some academicians had expressed a passing interest in painting of the 14th or 15th century, although few would have dared to suggest that it approached the sophistication of Raphael and his successors. At the beginning of the 1800s this prejudice began to wane. Wilhelm Heinrich Wackenroeder's essay, 'Outpourings from the Heart of an Art-Loving Priest', was published in 1797. The essays – in the form of a series of anecdotes – stressed that good painting was contingent upon spiritual devotion. The intellectual ideas of Winckelmann and other theorists and artists of the Enlightenment were abandoned in favour of a style of painting that expressed simply piety. Albrecht Dürer (1471–1528), a painter who worked in Germany, was seen as a perfect model. Dürer represented simple, God-fearing people in pictures painted in an equally simple and straightforward 'unlearned' manner. Similar sentiments had been expressed by Wackenroeder's contemporary, the philosopher and critic Friedrich von Schlegel. After an initial bout of philhellenism, Schlegel shifted his allegiance to the examples given by early Italian painting. Such paintings were, again, recognized as unsophisticated but nonetheless had, so Romantics believed, an impressive capacity to impart 'feeling', 'love', 'piety' and 'quiet enthusiasm'.

An enthusiasm for primitive Italian and Northern European painting first found practical form in the work of the *Lukasbrüder,* the Brotherhood of Saint Luke. The Brotherhood was established in 1809 by students who had recently left the Academy in Vienna. Dissatisfied by the pedantic academic curriculum, the group eventually fled Austria and established itself in the disused Benedictine monastery of Sant' Isidoro in Rome. Here Franz Pforr, Johann Friedrich Overbeck, Ludwig Vogel, Johann Konrad Hottinger, Joseph Sutter and Joseph Wintergerst attempted to revive something of the monastic life artists had led in the Middle Ages. The brethren described themselves as 'God's Workmen' and saw their mission as both religious and artistic, wherein the aim of painting was to excite devotion in both the painter and spectator. They further contended that sound painting was dependent upon an equally sound spiritual disposition and failed to understand how a dissolute life could possibly be reconciled with the production of worthy and especially of religious painting. It is interesting to note that Overbeck's piety was such that he found it appropriate to convert to Catholicism, the prime impetus behind many of the original paintings he so admired. Not all members of the Brotherhood embraced Catholicism, although they each tried to capture something of the monastic atmosphere of the Middle Ages. They worked, for instance, in the seclusion of converted cells and met in the refectory each evening to read and discuss their works. Some members of the group even adopted a pseudo-medieval style of dress. For example, Ford Madox Brown described a meeting with Overbeck in which the latter received him clad in a fur-trimmed cap and a black velvet habit tied about the waist with a long cord, dress commonplace in 15th-century Bruges.

The style of painting produced by the Nazarenes, as they later called themselves, varies. Some paintings evoke a naturalistic style popular in Germany and the Low Countries in the 15th and 16th centuries, while others depend heavily upon early Italian influence. Some pictures even employ a muddled perspective common in early Quattrocento paintings; others emulate the serenity of Raphael. Raphael, however, was about their most recent source of inspiration, for the Nazarenes were unanimous in their rejection of the gratuitous technical wizardry and vacuous subject matter of his successors. Furthermore, the brothers drew not with the broad, soft chalks used by the Old Masters and, by extension, the drawing classes at the academy, but used hard, sharp pencils that gave the artist an opportunity to depict subjects in meticulous detail. Peter von Cornelius, who had joined the Brotherhood in 1811, used precisely this detailed style in a series of illustrations, heavily influenced by the drawings of Albrecht Dürer, made for Goethe's *Faust*. Goethe, however, warned against Cornelius's rejection of the accepted Classical manner and his too-heavy dependence upon a nationalistic tradition.

Although the Brotherhood of Saint Luke lost much of its original impetus, its example did have a strong influence on British painting in the 1830s and 1840s, thus preparing the ground for the Pre-Raphaelites. English culture nursed an interest in medieval art and architecture since the middle of the 18th century, and this penchant began to increase drastically in the 19th century. Prince Albert was an active patron of the arts both as an amateur and in his official capacity as Consort to Queen Victoria. As a German prince, he had a patriotic affinity toward a Teutonic or Northern European Gothic style. The authority of this already popular style increased immeasurably when it was chosen as the appropriate idiom for Sir Charles Barry's new Houses of Parliament (designed with the assistance of Augustus Welby Northmore Pugin) in 1839. A royal commission, under the direction of Prince Albert, supervised the decoration of the palace, ordering a series of frescoes for its interior. The choice of fresco – painting with pigments onto wet plaster – as the medium is significant, for it was common in the Middle Ages and early Renaissance, but virtually extinct in 19th-century Britain. However, consistent with the vogue for medieval art and architecture, it was revived as a fitting manner for decorating Barry's Gothic palace. Peter von Cornelius was asked to advise the commission on the decorations, and envoys – among them Charles Eastlake and William Dyce – were dispatched to conduct research on the technique of fresco painting. Dyce was eventually commissioned to paint the frescoes and, with the assistance of Ford Madox Brown, completed five out of seven murals for the Queen's Robe Room, illustrating the apt chivalric themes of Religion, Generosity, Hospitality, Mercy and Courtesy.

The Pre-Raphaelite Brotherhood was established in the autumn of 1848 with the declamatory zeal of immature young men eager to tilt at the windmills of academic convention. It is important to recognize, however, that the Pre-Raphaelite credo that emphasized the importance of natural observation and heartfelt sentiment in painting, a sentiment found in abundance in the 14th and 15th centuries, was, in practice, one of a long series of broadsides made against academic establishments throughout Europe and party to a longstanding interest in medieval culture in Britain.

RIGHT *Peter von Cornelius*, The Last Judgement.

CHAPTER TWO

OF

REAL THINGS UNSEEN

THE PRE-RAPHAELITE BROTHERHOOD, 1848–1854

Ford Madox Brown, The Pretty
Baa-Lambs (detail). *First exhibited
at the Royal Academy in 1852.*

The Pre-Raphaelite Brotherhood was founded in London in September 1848. Initially a secret society, there were seven founder-members: Dante Gabriel Rossetti (1828–82), John Everett Millais (1829–96), William Holman Hunt (1827–1910), James Collinson (1825–81), FG Stephens (1828–1907), Thomas Woolner (1825–92), who was the only sculptor among the group, and William Michael Rossetti (1829–1919), a tax clerk by trade and the Brotherhood's secretary. Ford Madox Brown (1821–93) was an active and influential 'fellow-traveller' but never became a formal member of the Brotherhood.

The aims of the group are not easily summarized. Millais, Rossetti and Hunt, who were the Brotherhood's dominant figures, were aged 19, 20 and 21, respectively, in 1848 and would have had only a fragmentary grasp of the Romantic current of thought that had emerged in opposition to academic convention. Only Madox Brown among the Pre-Raphaelite circle had had first-hand experience of early Italian painting and only Hunt, it appeared, had cast an eye over Ruskin's *Modern Painters*. It is not surprising, then, to discover that the Brotherhood's credo was immature and at times confused. All three painters had been students at the Royal Academy and were bound primarily by a strong antipathy toward its institutionalized approach and an equally strong enthusiasm for art that rode roughshod over conventional taste. William Blake and William Hogarth, both of whom flouted academic convention, were admired by the circle, although it was early Italian and Flemish painting that had a special place in the Brotherhood's collective heart.

Several painters associated with the Brotherhood claimed to have invented the label 'Pre-Raphaelite' or, at least, to have explained its origin. Students at the Royal Academy had, apparently, used the term as a pejorative description of the early Italian art so admired by Millais and Hunt. There is evidence, however, that the term 'Pre-Raphaelite' had some currency well before 1848, although Millais and Hunt both claimed responsibility for the name. Writing in *Pre-Raphaelitism and the Pre-Raphaelite Brotherhood*, published in 1905, Hunt claimed that it was he who recommended the use of the term Pre-Raphaelite in preference to 'Early Christian', a label that had been used regularly by both Rossetti and Millais. The term 'Early Christian' would have had some unfortunate pro-Catholic connotations in mid-19th-century England and would have evoked some of the bitter

disputes between the Church of England and Tractarian factions centred around Oxford. Rossetti was responsible for appending the term 'Pre-Raphaelite' to the word 'Brotherhood', thus affording the society something of a conspiratorial and monastic air.

The earliest paintings associated with the Pre-Raphaelite circle used themes from medieval literature or the Bible. It is curious to discover, however, that members of the Brotherhood constantly stressed

James Collinson,
St Elizabeth of Hungary,
c. 1848–1850.

the importance of naturalism in painting. William Michael Rossetti attempted to summarize the aims of the Brotherhood and required only that painting be purged of rules; the logical formulae that had dogged the arts for centuries were to be abandoned for a canon that prescribed only nature's example and the artist's untutored intuition. These sentiments had been endorsed by Hunt. He had stressed the importance of nature as the prime source of reference for painters, and had roundly condemned the 'lethal' influences of academicians such as Le Brun, Mengs and Reynolds.

The Pre-Raphaelite concept of naturalism requires careful qualification. The movement, at least in its earliest stages, declined to represent the real, immanent world of the mid-19th century and its paintings are quite distinct from the naturalistic paintings being produced in France by artists such as Gustave Courbet.

Rather, the Pre-Raphaelites insisted that painters of the 14th and 15th centuries were unsophisticated craftsmen. Motivated only by simple piety and un-burdened with the theoretical trappings of later generations of painters, artists of the Trecento and Quattrocento were able to work with a direct and heartfelt simplicity and represent the world in an un-complicated, straightforward style. Pre-Raphaelite painters and their associates followed this example.

They used medieval or biblical subject matter but treated the themes with a marked sense of unsophisti-cated naturalism, wherein scenes from the past were depicted as real, historical events. Pre-Raphaelite paint-ings were often prepared only after a good deal of historical research into the customs, dress, furniture and accessories of the period. In fact, it was this same desire for verisimilitude in painting that eventually led Hunt to visit the Holy Land and paint religious pictures in the very environment where the scenes were supposed to have taken place.

The blend of archaism and naturalism that charac-terized many of the earliest Pre-Raphaelite pictures had been used by Ford Madox Brown several years before the foundation of the Brotherhood. In 1845 Brown began a work entitled *The Seeds and Fruits of English Poetry.* The picture, made in a form approxi-mating that of an early Italian triptych, shows Chaucer reading his poetry to Edward the Black Prince sur-rounded by courtiers and flanked by a pantheon of British poets. On the left-hand panel of the picture are Milton, Spenser and Shakespeare; on the right stand Byron, Pope and Burns. Set into roundels on either side are Oliver Goldsmith and James Thomson, and sleeping in the spandrels between the three arches are the Norman Troubador and the Saxon Bard, the two sources of inspiration behind British poetry. Putti

Sir John Everett Millais, Isabella, *1848–1849. The picture carries the inscription PRB on the base of Isabella's chair.*

lined along the base of the picture carry cartouches, each bearing the names of two British poets. They include: Campbell and Moore; Shelley and Keats; Chatterton and Kirke White; and Coleridge and Wordsworth. Although the subject is almost absurdly contrived and reminiscent of the nationalistic fervour found in some 18th-century art and architecture, the style of painting is nonetheless naturalistic. The bituminous colouring and theatrical composition found in some conventional paintings are exchanged for a brightly coloured and meticulously detailed arrangement of figures informally huddled around the central figure of Chaucer.

A similar sense of naturalism is found in Madox Brown's picture of *Wycliffe Reading his Translation of the New Testament to his Protector, John of Gaunt*, painted in the winter of 1848. The picture shows Wycliffe centrally positioned under a segmented arch, flanked by Chaucer and Gower on the left and John of Gaunt and the Duchess of Lancaster on the right. In the left- and right-hand corners of the picture are two allegorical figures representing the Protestant and Roman Catholic faiths. Although the painting is, again, contrived and betrays a debt to the Nazarenes, naturalism – albeit in an unusual form – is much in evidence. All of the figures within the picture were modelled by friends and associates of the artist. Brown's diary records that one 'Old Coulton' posed for the figure of Wycliffe and other figures within the picture are identified: his favourite model, Maitland, posed for John of Gaunt, Gower and the figure of Protestant Faith; one Mrs Ashley posed for the Duchess, and the child on her lap was modelled upon the artist's infant daughter. Brown's sense of naturalism also extends to the furniture and costumes: Henry Shaw's recently published *Specimens of Ancient Architecture and Dresses and Decorations of the Middle Ages* were consul-

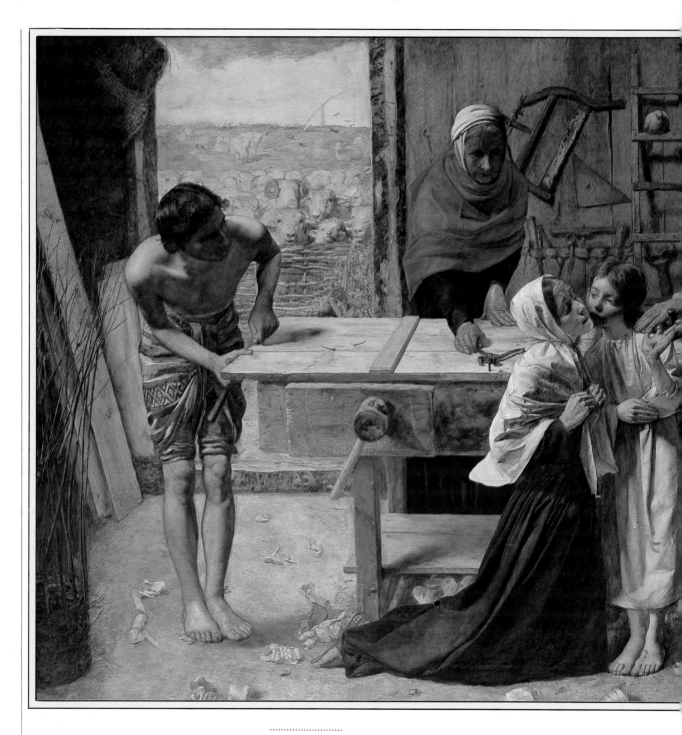

Sir John Everett Millais, Christ in
the House of His Parents,
*1849–1850. The scene from Christ's
childhood was inspired by Rossetti's*
The Girlhood of Mary Virgin,
painted during the previous year.

ted to ensure that the costume and furniture within the picture were historically appropriate to the period.

Madox Brown was a tutor to Rossetti and mentor to the Pre-Raphaelite Brotherhood, and his works betray many of the characteristics that are found in Pre-Raphaelite painting. But the first genuinely Pre-Raphaelite works were executed in the autumn and winter of 1848–49. They were by Rossetti, Millais and Hunt, and they bore the enigmatic inscription 'P.R.B.'

The pictures were Millais' *Isabella*, Hunt's *Rienzi Vowing to Obtain Justice for the Death of his Younger Brother* and Rossetti's *The Girlhood of Mary Virgin*. They have much in common and are quite distinct from some of the works by the same painters that immediately predate the formation of the Brotherhood. Millais' *Isabella* depicts a violent theme adapted by Keats from Boccaccio's *Decameron*, in which an ill-fated love affair between Isabella and Lorenzo ends in tragedy. Lorenzo, a servant in Isabella's household, was considered a poor match by her brothers and was promptly murdered. His ghost revealed the murder to Isabella who exhumed the body, severed the head and hid the memento in a pot of basil. The head was discovered and taken by Isabella's brothers, and Isabella herself eventually died of a broken heart. Millais' picture is painted in bright colours and drawn with meticulous attention to detail. Moreover, it is organized in a very unconventional manner, quite unlike the affected composition of *Cymon and Iphigenia*, painted the previous year. The figures are arranged around a table that sharply recedes into the distance. There is a curious absence of linear perspective in the painting; close inspection shows that all the figures are the same size, irrespective of their distance from the spectator. A contemporary critic, writing of *Isabella* in the *Literary Gazette*, recognized this characteristic and thought the absence of conventional perspective an impressive imitation of an 'Early Italian' manner.

Millais' *Isabella*, like the majority of early Pre-Raphaelite works, contains a strong narrative which is emphasized by objects or symbols that refer to some larger aspect of the literary source. Lorenzo passes Isabella a blood-orange served from a plate decorated with a scene from either the story of David and Goliath or that of Judith and Holofernes, both of which involve decapitation. On the balustrade in the background of the picture stands an ominous pot of basil beside which two passion flowers entwine.

A similar interest in prefigurative symbolism ap-

pears in Dante Gabriel Rossetti's first Pre-Raphaelite painting, *The Girlhood of Mary Virgin*. The picture, like *Isabella*, forsakes conventional perspective. Rossetti apparently found the subject tiresome and his lack of application is evident in the way in which the figures are, again, identical in size, irrespective of their position in the picture. Still, the painting is passably naturalistic, showing an adolescent Mary working at a piece of embroidery (Rossetti himself stated that the pastime would have been a likely one for young women of the period). Surrounding Rossetti's 'symbol of female excellence' are devices that prefigure the Virgin's fate. The angel clasps a lily, a symbol of purity, which is to be presented at the Annunciation. The dove on the trellis represents the Holy Ghost, the lamp stands for piety, and the vine bears fruit which, made into wine, symbolizes the sacrament of the Eucharist. It is worth remembering that the subjects of many Pre-Raphaelite pictures were quite original and that their often arcane symbolism would have eluded most spectators. In this instance, Rossetti explained the meaning of the components in the picture by means of a sonnet inscribed on the original frame. In the second verse Rossetti wrote:

> These are the symbols. On that cloth of red
> I' the centre, is the Tripoint, – perfect each
> Except the second of its points, to teach
> That Christ is not yet born. The book (whose head
> Is golden Charity, as Paul hath said)
> Those virtues are wherein the soul is rich:
> Therefore on them the lily standeth, which
> Is Innocence, being interpreted.
> The seven-thorned briar and the palm seven-leaved
> Are her great sorrows and her great reward.
> Until the time be full, the Holy One
> Abides without. She soon shall have achieved
> Her perfect purity; yea, God the Lord
> Shall soon vouchsafe His Son to be her Son.

The Brotherhood was initially encouraged by the way in which its first works had been received. The journal the *Athenaeum* had sniped at Millais' unconventional *Christ in the House of His Parents* and complained,

quite astutely it seems, that the work defied the accepted canon of beauty. Other critics, however, were more appreciative. Rossetti's *The Girlhood of Mary Virgin* received critical acclaim from many quarters and was bought by the Marchioness of Bath for the not inconsiderable sum of 80 guineas. Millais' *Isabella* sold for almost twice that sum and Bulwer Lytton, whose novel, *Rienzi, the Last of the Tribunes,* had formed the basis for Hunt's first Pre-Raphaelite work, wrote to the artist to express his deep admiration of the picture.

It was a growing sense of confidence brought on by such critical acclaim that led the Brotherhood to expand and articulate both its literary and artistic aims in the form of a magazine, first published in 1850 and entitled *The Germ*. The literary aspirations of the circle were summarized by William Michael Rossetti. Poetry should, he maintained, be the result of honest and personal convictions of the writer rather than determined by literary convention. The advice is, in fact, the equivalent of that given to painters, yet, despite Rossetti's dictum, it is difficult to discern any literary or theoretical party line within *The Germ*. FG Stephens, for example, under the pseudonym of Laura Savage, wrote an apologia for early Italian art and a curious defence of contemporary, industrial subject matter. John Lucas Tupper shared Stephens' (or rather, Savage's) interest in contemporary themes in painting, whereas John Orchard insisted that painting should be the vehicle for religious sentiment. *The Germ*, which ran to only four editions, also contained contributions from William Bell Scott, Ford Madox Brown, Coventry Patmore, Walter Howell Deverell, Christina Rossetti and others. It did much to swell the ranks of the Brotherhood beyond its initial secret seven. In the summer of 1850 the press and the public at large began to learn of the existence of the hitherto covert movement, and critical reactions to the circle began to take on a distinctly hostile turn.

Several Pre-Raphaelite pictures exhibited at the Royal Academy and at the Free Exhibitions in 1850 and 1851 were subject to bitter critical censure. Millais' *Christ in the House of His Parents* was savagely attacked by Charles Dickens in *Household Words* of 1850. Dickens described the figure of Christ as 'a hideous, wry-necked, blubbering, red-haired boy in a nightgown . . .' and his mother as '. . . so horrible in her ugliness that . . . she would stand out from the rest of the company as a monster in the vilest cabaret in France or in the lowest gin-shop in England.' *The Times*, the *Art Journal* and the *Literary Gazette* also took great exception to the painting, variously criticizing it for its deliberately archaic style and its ugliness.

Rossetti's *Ecce Ancilla Domini!*, a radical reinterpretation of the Annunciation in which the Virgin, dressed in white rather than blue, is shown reclining on a bed, was criticized both for its design and its presumptuous attempt to tamper with Church teaching. Hunt, shaken by the criticism directed at Rossetti's picture, omitted the Pre-Raphaelite insignia from *A Converted British Fami'y Sheltering a Christian Missionary from the Persecution of the Druids*, a contentious picture designed with an eccentric sense of perspective and riddled with dangerously ambiguous liturgical symbolism.

It is important to recognize that the critical attention given to the Pre-Raphaelite works exhibited in the early 1850s was often motivated not only by artistic doubts about reviving the archaic conventions of 14th- and 15th-century painting, but also by the covert nature of the Brotherhood and some of the curious religious affinities found in its works. Since the beginning of the 1830s, a militant High Church sect within the Church of England had made a concerted attempt to revive some of the rituals and traditions of the early Church. To some extent, this revival was a logical extension of the Romantic revivalism that had touched architecture, literature, social reform and, not least, painting and sculpture. Some preachers and theologians, however, had revived ritual as a counter to the spiritually vacuous service of the liberal Church establishment and had, as a consequence, moved increasingly close to the conventions of the Roman Catholic religion. The increasingly embittered debate between these High Church, or Tractarian, factions and the liberal establishment was exacerbated when militant Low Church Evangelists added their weight to the dispute. Thereafter, attitudes immediately began to polarize. John Henry Newman, vicar at St Mary's in Oxford and one of the most vociferous and articulate participants in the Oxford Movement, was silenced by his bishop and withdrew from public life until he eventually defected to Catholicism.

Conversions to Rome on the part of both clergy and laymen increased (James Collinson among them) and soon became the source of some public anxiety. What had once been a limited dispute among academics and theologians at Oxford had developed into a source of great public concern, with political ramifications on the traditional bond between Church and State in England. Public attention was so attuned to these issues that a religious picture with anything other than the most innocuous and conventional imagery would have immediately been seen to identify with one faction or another. It was in this context that some critics spotted a covert and dangerous Mariolatry within Ford Madox Brown's *The Pretty Baa-Lambs*, first exhibited at the Royal Academy in 1851. The painting, in fact, showed only a young woman with a child in her arms standing in the open air on a brilliant sunlit day feeding sheep. Some years later Brown was to set the record straight, explaining that 'a deep philosophical intention' was not his aim and that the painting was of 'a lady, a baby, two lambs, a servant maid, and some grass'.

The critical attention generated by the Pre-Raphaelite paintings of the early 1850s became important to the subsequent development of the circle. Attacks in the press prompted Coventry Patmore to seek the help of John Ruskin who came, albeit somewhat guardedly, to the Brotherhood's defence. Ruskin disassociated himself from their ill-chosen and contentious name and any High Church leanings within the Brotherhood's oeuvre, but staunchly defended their heightened sense of naturalism, even in such works as Collinson's flagrantly Romanist *Convent Thoughts* of 1851. Ruskin qualified his support in a series of letters to *The Times*, the first of which appeared in May 1851. He defended their pictures against specious accusations of an obsessive attention to often superfluous detail, and to charges of a self-conscious archaism and poor perspective.

Ruskin countered that the Pre-Raphaelite technique of illuminating the whole picture rather than simply its most significant parts was entirely consistent with the phenomenon of natural sunlight which, he claimed, had marginally greater authority than academic convention. The Pre-Raphaelites had, in fact, evolved a particular technique for achieving this effect of sunlit colour in their works. The technique, which Millais wanted to keep secret, involved the application of a thin layer of wet, white oil paint on the surface of the canvas, over which transparent layers of colour were added with a sable watercolour brush. When applied with sufficient care the white paint would shine through rather than mix with the pigment, affording the colour a particular brilliance.

Ruskin further argued that the perspective within Pre-Raphaelite pictures was not especially at fault and that he could find far greater errors in any 12 academic pictures chosen at random. The works of the

....
William Holman Hunt, A
Converted British Family
Sheltering a Christian Missionary
from the Persecution of the
Druids, *1850.*
....

Pre-Raphaelites were, moreover, archaic only in that they shared the same fidelity to nature as painters of the 14th and 15th centuries. The paintings were, he insisted, 'more earnest and complete in their aspirations than anything painted since the time of Dürer' and he suggested that the Brotherhood's efforts would eventually establish a school of art nobler than anything seen in the past 300 years.

Ruskin's support was an enormous boost for the Brotherhood and, through the medium of his correspondence – a pamphlet on the aims of the movement and subsequent editions of *Modern Painters* – he served to clarify the Pre-Raphaelite cause and associate it with an ever more assiduous attention to natural-

ism. The period between 1851 and 1854 was to a large extent the 'high noon' of Pre-Raphaelitism and saw the production of some impressive essays on natural-ism, particularly on the part of John Everett Millais.

In 1852 Millais painted a picture inspired by the fourth act of *Hamlet* in which Ophelia, driven mad by her lover's feigned insanity and the death of her father, casts herself into a stream. The picture contains an unprecedented attention to botanical detail. The figure of Ophelia, modelled by Elizabeth Siddal (posing in a bath of tepid water), is surrounded by plant life, much of which has a symbolic allusion in the text of Shakespeare's play. In 1852 the painting also contained a bunch of daffodils, although Tennyson pointed out that the presence of spring flowers was inconsistent with the other summer flora in the picture and Millais, for verisimilitude's sake, removed them. The aspirations of Millais and Ruskin meet more directly, however, in the artist's portrait of the critic, painted while the two were on holiday at Glenfinlas in Scotland. The picture shows a contemplative Ruskin standing on some magnificently detailed rocks beside a torrent and reflects the critic's profound interest in natural science.

Millais began to receive critical acclaim for many of his pictures and was elected an associate member of the Royal Academy in 1853. The works of Hunt and Rossetti had taken a different turn, however. Hunt's paintings, although intensely naturalistic, were increasingly laden with moral or religious messages. Some moral predicate had been an important part of the Pre-Raphaelite credo in 1848 and, although the individual interests of the brethren had broadened, Hunt believed that his work remained true to its original spirit. *The Awakening Conscience* and its pendentive, *The Light of the World*, serve as two good examples of Hunt's secular and spiritual interests in painting. The former picture shows a young, half-dressed (in Victorian terms) woman rising from the lap of her lover toward an open window, which is reflected in the mirror in the background of the picture. She is shown at the precise moment of her conversion from a dissolute and wanton existence as a kept woman to a state of redemption symbolized by a shaft of light on the right of the picture. Other components in the painting allude to the woman's plight: a cat is about to pounce on a bird under the table on the left of the picture; on the right is a glove cast off in a way that could prefigure her own fate. The two pieces of sheet music on the piano and floor are, respectively, Thomas Moore's *Oft in the Stilly Night* and Edward Lear's *Tears, Idle Tears*, both of which refer, appropriately, to lost innocence. *The Light of the World* shows spiritual redemption in contrast to worldly sin as epitomized in the popular Victorian image of the fallen woman. Ruskin explained the symbolism in the picture – which appeared to have gone completely above the heads of most spectators – in a letter to *The Times*. The disused and overgrown door on which Christ knocks is a symbol of the human soul ignorant or impervious to Christ's teaching, and the light from his lantern embodies conscience on the one hand and salvation on the other.

Meanwhile, Rossetti's paintings had assumed a form quite alien to those of his contemporaries. Paintings such as Hunt's *The Hireling Shepherd*, Brown's *The Last of England*, Deverell's *The Irish Vagrants* and Millais' *A Huguenot, on St Bartholomew's Day* had taken on a cross-section of social, religious and literary themes, although all had been expressed with a keen sense of naturalism. Rossetti, however, had not publicly exhibited a picture since 1850 and had evolved a personal and mystical symbolism inspired by chivalric themes and medieval poetry. His interest in mysticism was complemented by a curiously ethereal space in his pictures, at times reminiscent of the watercolours and drawings of William Blake, whom Rossetti greatly admired. Evidence of Rossetti's quite unnaturalistic use of space had been evident in his *Ecce Ancilla Domini!* In *The First Anniversary of the Death of Beatrice*, painted in 1853–54, Rossetti shows Dante interrupted by three friends who come upon him while he is drawing an angel to commemorate the death of his beloved Beatrice. Rossetti depicts a well-observed room (modelled upon a Flemish rather than Florentine interior) with a view across the Arno; the figures are again based on friends, family and associates. The final result, however, is far removed from the naturalism of his contemporaries, with vivid local colours and a very unconvincing picture space. Rossetti was to repeat the theme of Dante and Beatrice on many occasions, particularly after the death of his wife, Elizabeth Siddal, from which point Dante's relationship with Beatrice became a deeply felt metaphor for the artist's own exclusive and obsessive marriage.

By about 1854 the Pre-Raphaelite Brotherhood had lost much of its original momentum and purpose. Millais had argued for its dissolution on the grounds that its members were no longer united by a common bond. The Brotherhood had always been fuelled by enthusiasm rather than some common purpose and these disparate aims were becoming acutely apparent by the mid-1850s. Individual members also began to abandon the Brotherhood. Thomas Woolner, for instance, had left to prospect for gold in Australia as early as 1852, and James Collinson departed the following year to train for Holy Orders in a Jesuit monastery. Hunt, moreover, left for Egypt in January 1854 and Millais, having received official recognition from the Royal Academy, had somewhat lost his credibility as a dissident.

Although the formally constituted Brotherhood had all but vanished, a loose confederation of painters, centred around some of the founder-members of the Pre-Raphaelite circle, did much to develop and articulate some of its ill-defined interests. It is to them, and especially to the towering figure of John Ruskin, that one has to look to trace the subsequent development of Pre-Raphaelitism.

....
William Holman Hunt, The Light
of the World, *1851-1853. The
frame carries an extract from
Revelation 3.20, 'Behold I stand at
the door . . .'*
....

CHAPTER THREE

John Ruskin

Giotto, Madonna and Child
Enthroned.

John Ruskin, Zermatt, Switzerland, *watercolour.*

In a letter of 1868 Dante Gabriel Rossetti stated that John Ruskin had not established the Pre-Raphaelite school, as many people believed. Rossetti's interpretation of Ruskin's role is historically quite accurate: the Pre-Raphaelites evolved, at least during the first few years, quite independently of Ruskin's influence, and the two only discovered some common purpose after the critic's intercession on behalf of the Brotherhood in 1851. The figure of John Ruskin is, however, of seminal importance to the unfolding aims of the Pre-Raphaelite circle. His work did much to clarify and articulate some of the Brotherhood's often ill-defined ambitions and provided historical and theoretical reference points, not only for the Pre-Raphaelites but also for many other 19th-century artists, architects and craftsmen active throughout Europe and the United States.

John Ruskin was born in February 1819, the only child of a middle-class Scottish sherry merchant and his Evangelical wife. He was educated at Christ Church, Oxford, having already gained an early appreciation of art and architecture through his father. The family travelled extensively throughout Europe during Ruskin's youth, visiting collections of art. Even at this early stage, the young man betrayed a marked distaste for Italian Renaissance culture. Ruskin – with a Low Church distrust of Catholic excess that was later to affect much of his appreciation of art and architecture – thought St Peter's in Rome absurdly pompous and fit only for a ballroom. He appears to have found a far greater appeal in the Alpine scenes that had inspired picturesque landscape painters in the early part of the 19th century, a style that depended less upon academic convention and far more upon the careful observation of nature.

An affinity toward the unaffected depiction of the natural world was to emerge as a consistent feature of Ruskin's work and an important standard for his assessment of the work of others. In his autobiography, *Praeterita,* Ruskin recalled an incident in which he came across a sprig of ivy growing around a thorn

Photograph of John Ruskin.

stem while walking near Peckham in South London. He was so taken with the innate natural beauty of the plant that he realized that he had yet to learn to draw the natural world without some element of artistic contrivance. Ruskin made a study of the ivy and recounted that 'when it was done I saw that I had virtually lost all my time since I was twelve years old, because no-one had told me to draw what was really there'. The experience changed his entire attitude to drawing and, Ruskin later claimed, enabled him to begin to understand the element of naturalism within the works of the Pre-Raphaelites.

Ruskin's first work outlining his ideas on naturalism in painting found form in the first volume of the monumental *Modern Painters – Their Superiority in the Art of Landscape Painting to the Ancient Masters*, published in May 1843. The work had, in part, been inspired by Thomas Carlyle's book, *On Heroes and Hero Worship*. Ruskin had planned to write a heroic defence of modern landscape painting with a particular emphasis upon the work of Turner as a riposte to the philistinism of the British press. The *Literary Gazette* and the *Athenaeum* had made a series of puerile slights against the venerable figure of Turner, likening his technique to painting with chocolate, cream, egg yolk and currant jelly. In the preface to *Modern Painters*, Ruskin explained that he planned initially to reply in the form of a pamphlet, although the venture soon gained uncontrollable momentum and emerged as nothing short of a treatise. The first volume, one of five, runs to several hundred thousands of words, much of it in the declamatory style of a pamphlet.

Modern Painters was written almost in secret, without any professional advice from contemporary artists or critics. The form of the work is unsystematic and jumps back and forth from general principles of landscape painting to the various strengths and weaknesses of its exponents. These principles were, however, laid out quite clearly. Landscape painting is a language, Ruskin insisted. Its overriding aim is the representation of natural facts, and no amount of imagination or intellect on the part of the painter can atone for the absence of truth. Ruskin's concept of natural, factual truth is more complicated than it first appears. Dutch painters of the 17th century were well-known for their mimetic capacity, and in this respect they were able to represent the landscape of the Low Countries with an impressive accuracy and attention to detail. Ruskin, however, found the Dutch School wanting. They have the ability to paint with eloquence but, he insisted, have little to say. 'Most paintings of the Dutch School,' Ruskin wrote, '. . . are ostentatious exhibitions of the artist's powers of speech, the clear and vigorous elocution of useless and senseless words'. It is important to remember that whenever Ruskin referred to Nature and an artist's ability to record it accurately, he was invariably alluding to something much greater than the inanimate stuff of the world outside. For Ruskin, Nature had a divine origin and was invested with a profound sense of *gravitas;* it was subject to change and growth, and took on a character which could be benign and tranquil at one end of the scale and malign and ferocious at the other. Painters such as those of the Dutch School or, perhaps, Canaletto, who aspired to paint nature's physical form at the expense of its spiritual, were, for Ruskin, of limited capacity.

A profound belief in the authority of Nature also led Ruskin to castigate not only those who mechanically recorded what was before them but also those painters who depended upon their own intellect or imagination in preference to the visible reality of the natural world. Claude Lorrain, the paradigm of the genre of landscape painting – at least for the English connoisseur – was cited as painting a 'mass of errors from beginning to end' on the grounds that his pictures were theatrical generalizations of scenes taken from the pastoral poetry of the ancients and bore little resemblance to the appearance of nature. Having disposed of many of the most conspicuous figures of 17th-, 18th- and 19th-century landscape painting – among them Poussin, Claude, Constable and Gainsborough – Ruskin went on to cite those painters who had been able to invest their work with some grander

....
Aelbert Cuyp, View of Dordrecht.
....

purpose than mimetic ability alone. These included artists such as Samuel Prout, Copley Fielding and Samuel Cox, painters of modest watercolours who were surprised to discover themselves the subject of such critical attention.

Edwin Landseer's painting, *The Old Shepherd's Chief Mourner*, was acclaimed with even greater enthusiasm. Landseer's picture shows a sheepdog resting its snout on its dead master's coffin while the shepherd's discarded hat, crook, Bible and glasses are nearby. To modern eyes, the picture is an acrid example of Victorian sentimentalism; to the young Ruskin the picture embodied an impressive sense of naturalism motivated by a noble ideal. The picture, Ruskin insisted, 'stamps its author, not as the neat imitator of the texture of skin, or the fold of drapery, but as a Man of Mind'. Ruskin's critical faculties are, perhaps, redeemed by his appreciation of Turner. His pictures, Ruskin maintained, demonstrated an understanding of the natural, factual world to which he referred so frequently, although these facts are

rendered with a sense of *gravitas* transcending literal visual experience. Turner, for Ruskin, represented not the prosaic details of the sea, mountains and sky but their very depth, movement, height and volume. In fact, so profound was Turner's understanding of the poetic qualities of natural phenomena that his authority had intimidated contemporaries who had shown promise as younger men.

The first volume of *Modern Painters*, published pseudonymously by 'A graduate of Oxford', was well received. The work established Ruskin's reputation as a critic and was followed by a second volume in 1846. In this instance, Ruskin's interest in fidelity to nature, evident throughout much of his work, was grafted onto an increasing interest and awareness of the importance of early Italian painting. Ruskin had been influenced by Oxford contemporaries such as Sir Thomas Dyke Ackland, HG Liddell (Dean of Christ Church, Oxford, 1855-91) and George Richmond, who had independently developed an interest in the arts of the Trecento and Quattrocento. In addition,

....
*A B O V E Joseph Mallord William
Turner,* Agrippina Landing with the
Ashes of Germanicus, *1839.*
....
*L E F T Joseph Mallord William
Turner,* Burning of the Houses of
Parliament, *1835.*
....

he had read Rio's *De la Poésie Chrétienne,* Waagen's
Kunstgewerbe und Künstler and Kugler's *History of
Painting,* all of which asserted the importance of
'primitive' painting of the 14th and 15th centuries. An
interest in painters such as Cimabue, Orcagna, Fra
Angelico, Benozzo Gozzoli, Giotto and others had
been further stimulated by Ruskin's journey through
Lucca, Pisa and Florence in 1845.

In the second volume of *Modern Painters,* having
drawn upon his experience of Trecento and Quattrocento painting, Ruskin fashioned a historical schema
that did much to qualify his admiration for the art of
the period and link it to a continuing commitment to
the importance of naturalism in painting. Ruskin iso-
lated four 'Schools': those of 'Love', 'Great Men',
'Painting' and 'Errors and Vices'. The 15th-century
Florentine painter Fra Angelico occupies the prime
position within the 'School of Love'. Ruskin described
him as an inspired saint and, although his executive
power might have been limited, his painting was
motivated only by a religious faith that was expressed

without any artistic affectation. The 'School of Great
Men' included other painters of the Trecento and
Quattrocento, among them Giotto, Orcagna, Ghir-
landaio and Giovanni Bellini. Artists of the second
school did not, for Ruskin, have quite the refined
sanctity of Fra Angelico. They were nonetheless
motivated by religious convictions rather than artistic
interests and Ruskin was at pains to point out that the
spiritual art of the 13th and 14th centuries was more
wholesome than the secular work of subsequent eras.
They painted, moreover, with a simple and unaffected style rendering the natural world as an object of
Divine Creation rather than some artistic playground
for gratuitously inventive pictorial style. The first and
second schools were, in this respect, quite different to
the 'School of Painting' and the 'School of Errors and
Vices'. Painters in these categories appeared to have
lost any religious interest and were motivated by the
whims of fashion. Ruskin cited the example of a painting of St Catherine by the 16th-century painter Correggio, in which the hands of the saint were distorted.
The distortion, Ruskin explained, was not the result
of Catherine's state of mind but only the fancy of the
painter.

Ruskin's antipathy toward painting of the 16th
century was elaborated on in the third volume of
Modern Painters, specifically in his critique of the
Raphael cartoon of the *Charge to Peter.* The cartoon

shows the risen Christ handing the key to the kingdom of heaven to Peter; around him are the remaining Apostles. The group are dressed in decorous flowing Roman costumes, despite having just landed a miraculously large draught of fishes, and are shown against a genteel pastoral backdrop. Ruskin contrasted what he considered Raphael's hypocritical rendition of the scene with both an account in the Gospels and what he imagined the scene to have really been like. The fishermen, he argued, would have been wet and cold; they would have been dressed in clothes more appropriate to their work, and would have been depicted in the barren landscape of Galilee rather than that of the Roman countryside. 'The moment we look at the picture we feel,' Ruskin wrote, 'our belief in the whole thing taken away. . . . It is all a mere mythic absurdity, and faded concoction of fringes, muscular arms, and curly heads of Greek philosophers'.

John Ruskin's appraisal of painters both ancient and modern was not always consistent and a reading of the first three volumes of *Modern Painters* reveals some contradictions. It is possible, nonetheless, to discern within Ruskin's work a clear critical understanding of the history of art and its strengths and weaknesses in the second half of the 19th century. In essence, Ruskin argued that some time around the beginning of the 1500s the course of painting went awry and the fault was largely attributable to Raphael and his successors. Painters before Raphael had been preoccupied with spiritual issues and its exponents had rendered the world with a pious and unaffected simplicity, aiming only to articulate religious truths. Raphael had grossly distorted those truths to the extent that religious doctrine was represented with an ethereal refinement that distorted and denied the reality of the Gospels. The tradition of over-refined painting had been enshrined in academic teaching, the influence of which was still apparent in the 19th century. A handful of modern landscape painters had shrugged off the burden of the Renaissance and had painted the world not according to academic prescription but as it appeared. Moreover, they had aspired to capture within their pictures not simply literal appearance but something of the Divine intention that underpinned it.

Joseph Mallord William Turner,
Venice, Calm and Sunrise,
1842–1843.

It was on critical premises such as these that Ruskin defended – or rather co-opted – selected Pre-Raphaelite pictures and their painters to justify his own ideas. In a series of critical essays entitled *Academy Notes*, in the *Edinburgh Lectures*, and in subsequent volumes and editions of *Modern Painters*, Ruskin qualified the support he had first offered in *The Times* of 1851. Hunt's *The Light of the World* is singled out for special attention; the picture was, Ruskin insisted, 'the most perfect instance of expressional purpose with technical power, which the world has yet produced'. *The Scapegoat*, painted by Hunt on the shores of the Dead Sea, was applauded for its single-minded purpose, although Ruskin had reservations about the technique. Arthur Hughes, who had remained on the periphery of the Pre-Raphaelite circle, was in turn praised for an unconventional painting of the Nativity. Ruskin particularly liked the use of colour in the picture and the way an angel on the left was shown holding a lantern. Ruskin thought the prosaic detail a good example of practical Christian ministry. John Brett, an associate of Coventry Patmore, was influenced by Ruskin's own observations on Alpine landscape in the fourth volume of *Modern Painters*, and painted some impressive mountain scenes with minutely observed geological details, among them *The Glacier at Rosenlaui* and *Val d'Aosta*. Ruskin referred to the latter in *Academy Notes* of 1859, stating that the picture was 'just as good as standing on the spot' where it was painted.

Ruskin believed the Pre-Raphaelite circle, at its best, to have matched the achievements of the early Italian painters who preceded Raphael. The circle was not guilty of archaism; these artists had, in fact, rediscovered some essential truths in painting and it was hoped that the discovery would put academic doctrine aside for good. There was even evidence, Ruskin believed, to suggest that the fidelity introduced by the Pre-Raphaelites into their pictures of 1848 and 1849 was, after an initially unfavourable reception, having an influence on the paintings shown at the Royal Academy Summer Exhibitions.

There had been a series of moral imperatives running throughout Ruskin's writing on art, maintaining that a properly constituted picture should make one aware of some Divine presence through the medium of an attentive and factual rendition of the natural world. For this very reason, early Italian painting remained high in Ruskin's estimation. Subsequent works by Ruskin, notably *The Stones of Venice* and *The Seven Lamps of Architecture*, elaborated on the moral sanction of early art and architecture and upheld the example of the Middle Ages both as an artistic and social ideal. The notion is an especially important one and exerted a profound influence on Pre-Raphaelite art and design in the second half of the century.

John Ruskin, Watercolour Study of Rock Fragment with Quartz Vein.

Hand in hand with an admiration for the aesthetic honesty of the art of the Middle Ages went an increasing interest in the character of the society that produced it. The Industrial Revolution precipitated profound social changes during the first half of the 19th century within both the city and the countryside, serving to drastically polarize the distribution of wealth in Britain. On the one hand the *nouveaux-riches* middle-class industrialists applauded expansion, technical progress and aggressive free trade, and, through the medium of economists such as Adam Smith and the Manchester School, evolved an economic system that sought to justify the generation of wealth irrespective of the misery and deprivation left in its wake. On the other hand there emerged a body of critics that, for a wide variety of reasons, denied the value of unfettered progress and sought intellectual and emotional refuge in the ideal of a medieval past, a body that included Pugin, Carlyle and, notably, Ruskin.

In 1836 the architect and critic, Augustus Welby Northmore Pugin (1812–52), wrote a work entitled *Contrasts*, in which a town of the 15th century was compared to the same town 400 years later. Antiquarian studies of Gothic architecture and its relation to alternative architectural styles were commonplace in the mid-19th century. Pugin, however, contrasted not simply the two respective styles but also the two societies from which they emerged, concluding that the

Gothic idiom was altogether more wholesome and the result of Christian society bound by spiritual rather than material values. Thomas Carlyle similarly compared the depravity of the present with the shining example of a medieval past in *Past and Present*, written in 1843. In this and other essays, Carlyle railed at the mechanized sophistication of the 19th century and its influence in all aspects of industrial, economic, cultural and spiritual life, an influence in which 'Men have grown mechanical in head and in heart as well as in hand'. The antidote is, once again, found in the example of the medieval past. The Middle Ages, Carlyle maintained, fostered a community in which people were bound together not by the institutional or financial ties that preoccupied the present but by human bonds of duty, fidelity, mercy and charity overseen by a governing class of heroes, the model of which was to be found in the chivalric ideal of the medieval knight.

Ruskin shared this profound distaste for the present and used the medium of medieval architecture and the system under which it was made as an incisive critical tool with which to place into proper context

John Ruskin, Portrait of Rose la
Touche. *Ruskin's unhappy affair
with Rose la Touche, some thirty years
his junior, preceded his mental
collapse in early 1871.*

both ancient and modern buildings and the societies that produced them. His appreciation of architecture had much in common with his appreciation of painting. The main difference between the two was that the public medium of architecture had a wide influence, whereas the influence of painting was restricted to the drawing room. The Renaissance again signified the moment when European architecture fell from grace. Writing in the first chapter of the first volume of *The Stones of Venice*, published between 1851 and 1853, Ruskin stated that 'I have not written in vain if I have heretofore done anything towards diminishing the reputation of the Renaissance landscape painting. But the harm which has been done by Claude and the Poussins is as nothing when compared to the mischief effected by Palladio, Scamozzi and Sansovino.' For within Renaissance architecture was the root and the expression of 'certain dominant evils of modern times'.

The failings of Renaissance architecture and its causes are various. Ruskin noted with an astounding degree of tendentious zeal that nothing of architectural note had been produced since the division of the Christian Church. He was prepared to concede that while Protestantism was hardly conspicuous in the art and architecture generated in its service, the Catholic Church meanwhile had not shown itself capable of a single great conception since its separation from Protestantism. It was, however, the cold logic with which Renaissance buildings were constructed and the way that logic denied any individual human creativity to which Ruskin most objected. It is important to remember that the Classical tradition had insisted that buildings be determined by a series of mathematical proportions, which found form in the use of columns used to pace out the dimensions of a façade in much the same way that musical notes are used to pace out time within a musical stave. A column assumed precise proportions based on that of the human figure; it came in five differing types, or orders (Tuscan, Doric, Ionic, Corinthian and composite), each of which had to be applied in a set context.

Ruskin had argued, albeit rhetorically, that the Classical tradition in architecture had been so systematized that it would be possible to dispense with human architects altogether and employ machines to turn columns, according to prescribed measurements and proportions. The strict, rule-bound tradition was, he insisted, inimical to real imagination or invention. Such buildings were, moreover, further indict-

John Ruskin, The Matterhorn seen from the Moat of the Riffelhorn, *1849.*

....
John Ruskin, Watercolour study of
the Chapel of Santa Maria della
Spina, Pisa, *1845.*
....

....
John Ruskin, Study for Gothic
Window Tracery, *1848. The
drawing was made for the third plate
of 'The Seven Lamps of Architecture'.*
....

able on grounds of infidelity and pride. The original Classical model derived from pagan Greece and could consequently be considered inappropriate for a Christian culture. The pride of the Classical tradition was evident in the way in which Renaissance buildings were invariably made of stone rather than local materials and stood out from neighbouring domestic architecture. Ruskin maintained that the whole tradition could be dispensed with very much in the same way that one could do away with the Renaissance tradition of painting that had been enshrined within academies of the fine arts.

The Gothic architecture of the Middle Ages, by contrast, had not, so Ruskin concluded, been constrained by regulations, and it was this absence of constraint that pointed to the liberty afforded to medieval craftsmen. Whereas the Renaissance architect would have designed a building and handed over those designs to a mason who would, in turn, have carved

each stone according to the prescribed dimensions, his medieval predecessor would not, so Ruskin implied, have been subject to this division of labour. Medieval craftsmen had the opportunity to plan and decorate a building according to their creative impulse and their labour involved active thought. This aspect of medieval craftsmanship is evident in the way in which Gothic architecture assumed a variety of forms. They were, as Ruskin stated, 'changeful', and this changefulness evidenced both the creative human intellect at work and the way in which Christianity recognized the contributions of all human souls.

Gothic architecture clearly lacked the mathematical perfection found, say, in the ornament on a Classical temple or a Palladian villa, but this sense of imperfection was also seen as a symbol of intellectual liberty and the way in which Christianity had the capacity to indulge human imperfection.

Ruskin stated that Christianity exhorted the craftsman to:

> Do what you can, and confess frankly what you are unable to do; neither let your effort be shortened for fear of failure, nor your confession silenced for fear of shame. And it is, perhaps, the principal admirableness of the Gothic schools of architecture, that they thus receive the results of labour of inferior minds and out of fragments full of imperfection, and betraying that imperfection in every touch, indulgently raise up a stately and unaccusable work.

This exhortation of the creative and spiritual benefits of medieval labour was in stark contrast to working conditions of the mid-19th century. In the influential chapter of *The Stones of Venice*, entitled 'On Nature of Gothic', Ruskin contrasted the creative labour of the Venetian glassworker with that of his modern English counterpart. The former produced objects of some use, drinking glasses, cups and so on, inventing new and beautiful forms. The latter, by contrast, was involved in the mechanical production of perfectly clear and well-formed glass with no creative content and often no practical use whatsoever. Ruskin referred to the tacit slavery involved in the modern production of useless glass beads, each perfectly fashioned from industrially produced glass rods by the glassworker with 'an exquisitely timed palsy'. Ruskin was to make a similar point in his condemnation of the refined finish of the modern English interior. Perfection, in each instance, was the result of machine production and machine production required the inhuman appropriation of the creative capacity that resided in all human souls. Sound design was contingent upon three basic requirements: invention and utility; the absence of perfection and finish for its own sake, and originality in the design.

The aesthetic and social example of the Middle Ages developed into a critique of Industrialism. Not only had creative ingenuity been all but snuffed out in the service of efficiency and profit, but the English countryside had been deployed as an enormous economic resource. In a lecture entitled 'The Two Paths', given in Edinburgh in 1859, Ruskin observed that he was unable to travel more than a thousand yards between Rochdale and Bolton Abbey without coming across a furnace; he wondered where the juggernaut of Industrialism would stop and asked rhetorically whether all of the native resources – the mountains and lakes of the north and west; the clay and chalk of the south – might not be used for some industrial purpose. If this was to be the case, the future of the arts in England – arts, which, of necessity, must be informed by the example of Nature – was bleak.

In 1871 Ruskin attempted to establish a counter to the excesses of industrialization with the foundation of the Guild of St George. In the second half of the century there were a number of articulate critics of the prevailing economic creed of *laissez-faire* utilitarianism – among them Marx, Engels, the Chartists and Christian Socialists – yet it is significant that Ruskin declined to embrace the levelling ambitions of the political left and referred instead to the social ideals of the distant past in the form of a pseudo-medieval guild. The foundation of Ruskin's Utopian community was announced in a series of letters to the labourers and workmen of Britain, published between May and August 1871 and entitled the *Fors Clavigera*. The Guild was to appeal to anyone sufficiently disaffected by modern society to want to establish some alternative. It was to be sustained primarily by agriculture without the aid of machinery, together with donations by affiliated guildsmen active in the outside world.

Ruskin had intended that the fraternity would spread throughout England and beyond and establish a social alternative to Industrial Capitalism. In fact, the success of the guild was limited to a handful of communities in Wales, Yorkshire and the Isle of Man. Although the Guild of St George was unsuccessful, the principles on which it was based were of inordinate importance to artists, craftsmen and architects active in the second half of the 19th century. These included the 'second wave' of Pre-Raphaelites who had gathered around Rossetti and Morris, first in Red Lion Square in London and later at the so-called 'Palace of Art', Red House in Bexleyheath, Kent.

CHAPTER FOUR

FROM

OXFORD TO SODOM

PRE-RAPHAELITISM IN THE 1850s AND 1860s

John Brett, The Val d'Aosta, *1858.*
First exhibited at the Royal Academy
in 1859.

Sir Edward Coley Burne-Jones,
Dorigen of Britain Waiting for
the Return of her Husband,
1871.

By the mid-1850s, the purpose of the Pre-Raphaelite Brotherhood seemed to be in question: there had been defections and resignations; founder-members such as Millais had doubted its *raison d'être* and had increasingly lost any sense of common purpose with his comrades; Hunt had left for the Holy Land, and there now appeared to be little consensus in style in the works of the original brethren. In 1854, however, Edward Coley Burne-Jones (1833–98) and William Morris (1834–96) had learned of the movement's work while at Oxford through *The Germ* and Ruskin's *Edinburgh Lectures,* and Pre-Raphaelitism, now centred around the charismatic figure of Rossetti, attracted some enthusiastic and influential converts to its cause.

Burne-Jones and William Morris had originally met at Oxford in 1853. Both had been profoundly affected by the cult of medievalism that was especially virulent in the university milieu. During their early days at Oxford, they had been avid readers of such medieval 'romances' as Alfred Lord Tennyson's *Morte d'Arthur,* Charlotte M Yonge's *The Heir of Redclyffe* and

Sir Kenelm Digby's manual for the latter-day knight, *Broadstone of Honour,* a text which, apparently, never left Burne-Jones's bedside. The two appear to have taken their interest in medievalism quite seriously. They had both intended to take Holy Orders and, with the support of their fellow student Cormel Price and Morris's considerable private income, to establish a monastic order dedicated to Sir Galahad. Neither ordination nor the monastery ever came to fruition although the pair's enormously high regard for the Middle Ages as an artistic and social alternative to the course of modern society never remained in doubt and was to exert a marked influence on their respective careers.

William Morris, having abandoned the plan to enter the priesthood, joined the architectural practice of George Edmond Street in 1856. It was during this

William Holman Hunt, The
Scapegoat, 1854. First exhibited at
the Royal Academy in 1856.

period that Burne-Jones, having long nursed a secret desire to become an artist, contacted his hero, Dante Gabriel Rossetti, at the Working Men's College in London. Rossetti was flattered by the attention and was to exert so powerful an influence over both Burne-Jones and Morris that the two were persuaded to abandon their respective architectural and academic careers and to take up painting. Rossetti had summarily declared that all other methods of expression had run their courses; poetry had reached its peak in the work of John Keats and, he advised, 'If any man has any poetry in him he should paint'. Working under the close guidance of Rossetti, Burne-Jones and Morris shared the top floor of his studio at Red Lion Square and began to paint. Some Burne-Jones drawings from this early period show the extent of Rossetti's influence, and, although the works are clearly derivative, they demonstrate a clear facility for painting that was to mature over the next two decades. Morris, by contrast, had a less obvious talent that is painfully evident in his few remaining paintings and drawings.

Among the earliest works undertaken by the new converts to the Pre-Raphaelite circle (or, more specifically, to Rossetti's circle) were the decorations for some pieces of furniture for the house at Red Lion Square. In 1856 Morris had designed a characteristically 'medieval' settle that had been made by a local carpenter and decorated, with Rossetti's help, with scenes from the poetry of Dante and Malory. The scheme is an interesting one and prefigures Morris's concern with the applied rather than fine arts by some years.

During the following year Burne-Jones, Morris and Rossetti went up to Oxford to assist in another collaborative scheme, the decoration of the Oxford Union. Benjamin Woodward, a friend of Rossetti's and a devotee of Ruskin, had designed the Union debating chamber and suggested that members of the Pre-Raphaelite circle might care to decorate its interior. Rossetti mustered a group of enthusiastic acolytes, including Morris, Burne-Jones, Arthur Hughes, Philip Webb, Val Prinsep, Hungerford Pollen, Spencer Stanhope, Alexander Munroe and the mathematics don, Charles Faulkner, many of whom had no professional painting experience. The cycle was to include 10 scenes from the *Morte d'Arthur* executed in the appropriately medieval medium of fresco. Variously modelling for one another in the guises of Sir Tristram,

Sir Lancelot and Sir Palomydes and others, the group undertook the programme with great enthusiasm. Morris had a suit of armour and a helmet made as props for the fresco by a local blacksmith, and even went so far as to wear the costume to dinner. His contribution to the cycle, executed with enormous speed but apparently limited technical dexterity, showed a scene entitled *Sir Palomydes' Jealousy of Sir Tristram,* with the figures partly eclipsed by enormous sunflowers. Little, however, remains of the cycle. Few of its executors knew anything about painting and even fewer knew about the medium of fresco. The cycle, which remained unfinished, deteriorated rapidly.

A better insight into Morris's fine art of the period is provided by his only extant oil painting, that of *Queen Guenevere* (sometimes called *La Belle Iseult*), painted in 1858. The painting shows Jane Burden, one of a handful of attractive female associates of the Brotherhood (collectively known as 'Stunners'), in the guise of King Arthur's consort. She stands before a crumpled bed that alludes to her adulterous love affair with Sir Lancelot, a theme upon which Morris was to elaborate in a volume of poems, *The Defence of Guenevere,* published in 1858. From a technical point of view, Morris's *Queen Guenevere* leaves much to be desired. The picture, like most Pre-Raphaelite works, is painstakingly painted, but in this instance done with little obvious flair save for the minute attention to the patterns on the tapestry, fabrics and costumes. Morris apparently loathed the final result. He was keenly aware of the limitations of his own ability and eventually abandoned the work, first giving it to Madox Brown, then to Rossetti.

The theme of medieval romance dominated the circle's work of the period. Around 1859 Rossetti had finally abandoned *Found,* one of his few paintings with an explicitly moral theme (in this instance, that of the fallen woman), and seemed thereafter to have concentrated on subjects from medieval poetry. *Paolo and Francesca,* a watercolour painted in 1855, is a good example. The picture takes its subject from Canto V of Dante's *Inferno* and uses a narrative composition of three sections. Paolo and Francesa are engaged in a worldly embrace in the left-hand panel, whereas in the right they atone for their adulterous relationship as they drift entwined through the flames of hell. In the central panel Rossetti depicted Dante and Virgil clasping one another's hands while looking mournfully to the infernal scene on the right.

ABOVE *Dante Gabriel Rossetti,* Pencil Portrait of Ford Madox Brown, *1852.*

RIGHT *William Morris,* Queen Guenevere, *1858. Morris' only extant oil painting was eventually abandoned and later completed by Rossetti and Madox Brown.*

Dantis Amor, painted in the year Rossetti finally abandoned *Found,* is executed in a similar idiom. The picture (which was originally part of the decoration for Morris's settle referred to earlier in the chapter) shows an allegorical figure of Love (Amor) holding a crescent dial on which the day and hour of Beatrice's death are inscribed. The picture is divided diagonally into two parts with Amor in the middle: one section contains the image of Christ inserted into a motif of the sun; the other shows Beatrice inserted within the crescent of the moon. The highly symbolic composition, strongly reminiscent of the work of William

....
A B O V E Philip Webb, The Red
House, *1859–1860. The home of
William and Jane Morris between
1860 and 1865.*
....
L E F T Dante Gabriel Rossetti, King
Rene's Honeymoon.
....

Blake, represents Beatrice's death and her transition from earth to heaven, as well as what Rossetti believed to be the central theme of both the *Vita Nuova* and *The Divine Comedy:* the notion that Love is the primal spiritual force in the universe.

Medieval romance took an altogether different turn in the unfolding career of William Morris. In 1859 Morris married Jane Burden, the model of his *Guenevere,* and in the following year they moved from London to the small village of Upton, near Bexleyheath in Kent. Philip Webb (1831–1915), who started out with Morris in GE Street's architectural practice, designed a large country house for the couple in a style quite unlike that of most contemporary Victorian buildings. As Morris was later to observe in his lecture, 'The Revival of Architecture', most houses of the period were designed in two or perhaps three styles: the classical, the Gothic or the '... utilitarian brick box with a slate lid which the Anglo-Saxon generally in modern times considers as a good sensible house with no nonsense about it'. In the Red House, however, Webb had managed to come up with an alternative idiom that was to exert a powerful influence on the vernacular tradition in domestic architecture for the next 50 years.

The style of Red House alludes to a medieval precedent, yet it is quite distinct from the absurdly over-decorated designs that often characterized the Victorian High Gothic Revival. The building is constructed in traditional red brick with a steeply pitched tile roof and is laid out within an orchard on a right-angled plan, giving the house something of the feel of a monastic cloister. It is interesting to observe that the style of the house has much of the Old World ruggedness and practicality that Morris so admired in the Great Coxwell Barn in Oxfordshire, often cited by Morris as the quintessence of medieval functionalism.

The interior of Red House was equally practical:

Portrait of William Morris,
*attributed to Charles
Fairfax-Murray.*

William Morris, Chair in ebonized
wood. *Upholstered in original
woollen tapestry with bird motif.*

the walls were white-washed, the floors tiled, and the main room on the first floor was left open to the roof, in order to render the construction of the roof clearly visible. Edward and Georgiana Burne-Jones, Madox Brown and his wife, Algernon Swinburne, Rossetti, Faulkner and others were regular visitors to the house and many helped to decorate and furnish it. Burne-Jones planned a series of tempera paintings and designed some pieces of stained glass for the house. He had also decorated a magnificent wardrobe with scenes from Chaucer's 'Prioress' Tale', which was given to Jane and William Morris as a wedding present. Jane Morris had embroidered some heavy serge drapes with daisy motifs that later found form in one of Morris's first wallpaper designs. Jane, together with her husband and Rossetti, had also decorated the ceiling with various motifs, the latter painting the motif 'As I cant' a mischievous inversion of Morris's adopted motto 'Si Je Puis'.

Red House was a hive of creativity on the part of a number of Pre-Raphaelites and their associates, although Morris's cherished ambition that the house would become the focus of a pseudo-medieval artistic community was not shared by his contemporaries and

the plan came to nothing. There emerged from the house, however, a more practical alternative to Morris's initial romantic vision. From the somewhat ill-conceived notion that artists of the Middle Ages concerned themselves not just with painting but with many other crafts besides, there evolved the more worldly venture of 'Morris, Marshall, Faulkner and Company, Fine Art Workmen'. The 'Firm', as the venture was popularly known, was established in April 1861 under the direction of Morris, Faulkner and PP Marshall (a surveyor and friend of Madox Brown), with Burne-Jones, Rossetti, Webb and Madox Brown as participants and holders of nominal £1 shares in the company. In reality financed by Morris's mother with an advance of £100, the Firm issued a prospectus and declared itself capable of undertaking virtually any 'species of decoration', including mural painting and the production of furniture, stained glass, metal-work and embroidery.

It is important to recognize that a marked shift in attitude had begun to occur with the foundation of Morris's company. Earlier Pre-Raphaelite ventures had often used medievalism as a shelter from the horrors of modern society, a disposition that is far

....
Ford Madox Brown, Adam and
Noah. *Stained-glass design made for
Morris and Company, 1865.*
....

....
Dante Gabriel Rossetti, Christ, St
Mary Magdalen and the Virgin.
*Stained-glass design made by Morris
and Company for All Saints, Selsley,
Gloucester.*
....

from uncommon among 19th-century romantics. The aim of the Firm, however, was more ambitious, in that it sought social reform through the medium of the decorative arts. Morris and Company was, like its romantic contemporaries, attracted to the culture of the Middle Ages, but used an essentially Ruskinian understanding of medieval art not as some romantic refuge but as an antidote and alternative to the shortcomings of present-day industrial society.

The applied arts of Industrial Capitalism had enjoyed their finest hour during the Great Exhibition of 1851, which Morris had steadfastly refused to visit. He declared instead a 'holy warfare against the age' and later, through the medium of the Firm, he and his colleagues began to craft an alternative to gratuitously decorative and meretricious mass-produced

efforts of the design industry at large. The Firm's products were (mostly) hand-made by caring artists and craftsmen who – like their medieval forbears – were able to delight in work that had not been subjected to the division of labour necessitated by mechanized production.

Morris's transition from 'romantic to revolutionary', as EP Thompson has observed, was a protracted one, although it is important to recognize the revolutionary potential of the principles of undivided and pleasurable work upon which Morris and Company was predicated. The Firm continued to produce a wide range of furnishings until it went into liquidation during World War II. Morris's interest in the company, however, began to waver. He increasingly came to realize that the applied arts could not precipi-

I am a king and chief · now am the tree barks thief ·

ever twixt trunk and leaf · chasing the prey ·

William Morris, Woodpecker.
Tapestry incorporating two lines of
Morris' verse, 1885.

tate the changes in industrial society he desired. The marked shift referred to above was to continue, for he was eventually to embrace the more thorough-going principles of Marxism and fashion a political rather than artistic programme in which, it was hoped, the mindless drudgery and ugliness of 19th-century Industrial Capitalism would be challenged by the dignified and undivided labour of the modern proletariat, the spiritual successors of the craftsmen of the Middle Ages.

The diversity of the Pre-Raphaelite oeuvre during the 1850s is demonstrated by the varying interests of those brethren who remained outside Rossetti's influence. The continuation of another important aspect of Pre-Raphaelitism's original creed, in many respects diametrically opposed to the medievalizing fancies of Burne-Jones, Morris and Rossetti, is found within the work of William Holman Hunt.

Hunt was never well-disposed toward the medieval revival that had touched his comrades. He had declined to work on the Oxford murals and spoke derisively of the vain attempt to decorate the Union on the part of artists of little proven skill and with no technical grasp of the specialist medium of fresco. Both Hunt and Millais also resented the extent to which Rossetti's peculiarly romantic and sensual brand of Pre-Raphaelitism, underwritten by Ruskin's critical influence, had, at least in the public's mind, appropriated the movement as a whole. Decades later, Hunt was to attempt to dissociate Rossetti from the true spirit of the movement in an essay, 'The Pre-Raphaelite Brotherhood: a Fight for Art', written in 1886. The true spirit to which Hunt referred found form not in flights of romance but in high-minded piety forged with an aggressive naturalism. Like Ruskin – from whose *Modern Painters* Hunt had evolved this extreme sense of naturalism – he believed that painting should aspire to some divine purpose, yet, like Ruskin, he took exception to the manner in which religious painting had invariably sought to mask divine truth behind artistic convention. It was, for Hunt, but a short step from some of the radical reinterpretations of the Gospels undertaken by the circle in 1848 and 1849, to the task of recovering the archaeological remnants of the Bible by painting religious art in the Holy Land itself.

Financed by the sale of *The Light of the World* (it fetched £400), Hunt left for Palestine in 1854, despite the counsel of his friends who greatly feared for his safety. In February he arrived in Cairo, where he painted *The Lantern-Maker's Courtship*, a secular picture of an over-ardent lantern maker attempting to unmask his prospective bride. A catalogue entry for the Royal Academy explained that it was commonplace for Muslim men to be able to see a woman's face fully only after marriage. The work had a didactic purpose in that it was partly an attempt to use the medium of painting to spread knowledge of other cultures and, Hunt explained, partly a 'trial of the question of getting models'. In this instance Pre-Raphaelite verisi-militude had run headlong into Islamic culture's aversion to figure painting.

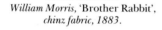

William Morris, 'Brother Rabbit',
chinz fabric, 1883.

William Morris and Edward Burne-
Jones, When Adam Delved and
Eve Span. *Frontispiece for Morris'*
'The Dream of John Ball', 1884.

Both *The Lantern-Maker's Courtship* and *The After-glow in Egypt,* an allegory of abundance, were made in preparation for far more ambitious pictures. In May 1854, Hunt, accompanied by the painter, Thomas Seddon, arrived in Palestine; in July he began *The Finding of the Saviour in the Temple,* the first religious picture to be painted in the location where the incident was thought to have taken place. The subject – Christ's discovery in the temple by Mary and Joseph as recounted by Luke in the second chapter of his Gospel – was informed by extensive research into the writings of the Jewish historian Josephus, the Bible, the Talmud and John Lightfoot's mid-17th-century study on Hebraic ritual, *The Temple Service as it Stood in the Dayes of our Saviour.* In addition, Hunt had visited synagogues and attempted to use only Semitic models (although this posed some difficulty as the local Jewry thought him part of an Anglican mission and themselves as breaking the second of the Ten Commandments). The work progressed very slowly, with some of the figures, Mary and Christ for instance, being painted on Hunt's return to England in 1856; as yet incomplete, the painting was eventually put to one side.

Shortly after having postponed work on *The Finding of the Saviour,* Hunt left Jerusalem for the treacherous journey to Usdam (called Oosdoom by Hunt), on the shores of the Dead Sea, to begin *The Scapegoat.* The source for the picture is an obscure one. It comes from Chapter XVI of *Leviticus* and refers to a Hebraic custom whereby two goats are selected as penitential symbols of human sin. On the Day of Atonement custom decreed that one goat was to be presented to the temple and the other, after a long period of vilification whereby the animal would be generally beaten, kicked and spat upon, was eventually driven into the wilderness and sacrificed. Hunt's picture shows the sacrificial goat, depicted against the lifeless saline shores of the Dead Sea on a site that was believed to be the location of the city of Sodom. Here, there is an intentional link between the city's misdemeanours and those sins invested in the figure of

Dante Gabriel Rossetti, St
Catherine, *1857. Made for Ruskin,
the St Catherine was the only oil
painting made by Rossetti between
1850–1859.*

Dante Gabriel Rossetti, The
Wedding of St George and
Princess Sabra, *1857.*

Dante Gabriel Rossetti, Arthur's Tomb, *1854.*

the goat. Hunt extends the allusion even further with a reference to Christ's own sacrifice for human sin, and his redemptive spirit symbolized in the picture by the rainbow on the right. The painting was executed from sketches made on location at Usdam – where, incidentally, Hunt's goat ailed and eventually died – and partly in Jerusalem. Hunt's mind-bending desire for naturalism was such that he even took supplies of earth back to the city where, having dried out a solution of mud in a tray in the hot sun, he then walked his replacement goat over the earth to achieve precisely the cracked and parched appearance of the shores of the Dead Sea.

The Scapegoat, despite Hunt's almost superhuman efforts, was not well received at the Royal Academy Exhibition of 1854. Ruskin had given the picture only qualified praise; the public at large was apparently mystified by the imagery which had no obvious precedent in European painting, and the press was critical. The Art Journal was very unsympathetic to Hunt's work and had dubbed him, derisively, the 'high priest' of the movement. The observation, perhaps fortuitously, was an astute one, for Hunt's Finding of the Saviour and Scapegoat had taken Pre-Raphaelitism to its ultimate conclusion. The original requirement that art should study nature attentively and have genuine ideas to express had assumed within Hunt's work the status of pictorial evangelism, demonstrating that the life of Christ and the Gospels were real historical events tethered to a specific geographical locale. It is, in many respects, difficult to think of a more assiduous, attentive and pious student of nature than Hunt.

The influence of Pre-Raphaelitism and, more specifically, Ruskin's interpretation of it, spread as other painters, largely on the periphery of the Pre-Raphaelite circle, began to adopt a naturalistic style. Henry Wallis, a friend of Arthur Hughes', painted The Stonebreaker in 1857, following the success of another painting on the theme of death, his Chatterton, exhibited in 1856. The minutely detailed former picture showed an exhausted labourer slumped dead against a mound of earth and referred to the practice of stonebreaking as a means of employment for destitute labourers. The picture was exhibited at the Royal Academy in 1858 and carried a quote from Carlyle's Sartor Resartus, wherein the author referred to both the sanctity of labour and its 'defacements' (of which stonebreaking was one) in contemporary society.

The theme of rural labour also appeared in John Brett's The Hedger. Inspired by Wallis's picture and the poor critical reception of his Val d'Aosta, Brett began a more animated study of nature. Ruskin had criticized his mountain landscape for its absence of 'feeling' and had made the general observation that no Pre-Raphaelite had yet undertaken a painting on the theme of Spring. Brett thereby went on to produce the detailed study of a Kentish landscape in May, animated with a woodcutter and his daughter in the background; the picture received critical acclaim from all quarters. It is interesting to note that Ruskin's passing comment, made after the Royal Academy Summer Exhibition of 1858, also generated other paintings of springtime, including Madox Brown's The Pretty Baa-Lambs, Millais' Apple Blossoms, and works on a similar theme by Hughes and Inchbold.

Perhaps the most famous picture on the subject of the Victorian preoccupation with labour is Ford Madox Brown's ambitious allegory, Work, painted between 1852 and 1863. The painting – which Brown annotated with a lengthy essay on the subjects and their significance – catalogued the various manifestations of labour in mid-Victorian England, rounded up, in this instance, beside the excavation that took place for the laying of water pipes at Heath Street, Hampstead, a northern suburb of London.

It had been common for 19th-century artists to paint picturesque shepherds, peasants or fishermen. Good, honest, manual toil, in an urban rather than a pastoral setting, had not quite accorded with refined Victorian sensibilities. Some commentators, however, had begun to initiate a change in the way in which labour and labourers were classified in contemporary society. Carlyle, Ruskin and later Morris had emphasized the spiritual and moral value of manual work. For Carlyle labour had been classified almost as a sacrament and man's very raison d'être. Ruskin, in turn, had qualified labour as a fundamentally creative activity through which men and women could express the essence of their humanity. Morris had progressively formed a vision – best expressed in his Utopian novel, News From Nowhere – in which hand-crafted, undivided labour would form a social order to challenge Industrial Capitalism.

In addition, the Victorian working classes were increasingly viewed as a potent force for social change.

....
RIGHT William Holman Hunt,
The Lantern-Maker's Courtship,
1854–1856. Exhibited at the Royal
Academy in 1861.
....

Ford Madox Brown, Work,
1856–1863. First exhibited in 1865.

For Marx, the proletariat had been seen as a potentially revolutionary force that would one day sound the death knell for capitalism. Less thoroughgoing reformers – the Christian Socialists and the Young England Movement, for instance – had dreamed of a quasi-feudal alliance between the working classes, the gentry and the Church as a united front against the upstart *nouveaux-riches* radicals of the Manchester School. The virile image of manual work had, as a consequence, a resonant appeal for many Victorians, and the navvy in Brown's picture – more in the mould of the benign yeoman than the Marxist revolutionary – literally emerges as the picture's 'hero'.

The heroic navvy in Brown's *Work* is flanked by people of various stations in Victorian society: on the left side of the picture is a poor flower seller; on the extreme right stand two 'Sages' – 'the cause of well-ordered work and happiness in others'. These sages are, appropriately, FD Maurice, the Christian Socialist and founder of the Working Men's College, and

Carlyle, whose lament for the bonds between social classes in pre-industrial society, *Past and Present,* inspired Brown's picture. Toward the top of the painting Brown has also included the rich who do not need to work. He refers to the pretty, carefree, wealthy young woman on the left almost in terms of a memento *mori,* warning that health and beauty eventually fail and cannot readily be bought.

At the opposite extreme of the social spectrum are the group of orphans marshalled by their 10-year-old elder sister in the foreground, and the idle labourers under the shade of the tree on the extreme right of the picture. To the left walking up Heath Street, is a pastry-cook with a loaded tray on his head; he is a symbol of society's surplus wealth. Class antagonism is even evident in the way in which the orphan's faithful mongrel and the pampered whippet are about to face up to one another.

Also portrayed in *Work* is an earnest young woman distributing religious tracts. The picture only found a patron, one TE Plint, four years after its inception, and he sponsored the painting on the condition that the moral and religious aspects of labour be emphasized. Brown thus inserted the downward-looking

....
John Brett, The Stonebreaker,
*1858. One of several works by Brett
in which the theme of Labour is used
to animate the natural landscape.*
....

female figure between the principal navvy and the wealthy woman behind the flower seller. The woman is handing out a pamphlet worded 'The Hodman's Haven, or drink for thirsty souls'.

Many of the seminal works of British Pre-Raphaelite painting had already been made by the mid-1860s. The circle's marked disposition toward artistic truth had perhaps seen its finest hour in Hunt's pictures made in Palestine. The movement's equally marked interest in medievalism had been elaborated first in Rossetti's paintings and poetry and later in Morris's experiment at Red House and the founding of Morris, Marshall, Faulkner and Company. Pre-Raphaelitism in England deserves a further chapter charting the unfolding careers of Rossetti and Burne-Jones, both of whom continued to effect a deeply personal ethereal style, and also the career of Millais who, under financial pressure, increasingly ingratiated himself with the social and artistic establishment.

Pre-Raphaelitism, usually considered a quintessentially British movement, had in the meantime spread to the United States. Ruskin's low church aesthetic and his emphasis on naturalism in preference to historical precedent had a strong appeal to a nation with a well-established tradition of religious independence and little chronological history. It is, then, to the United States that one has to turn for the following stage in the history of the movement.

CHAPTER FIVE

'NO PAST, NO MASTERS, NO SCHOOLS'

RUSKIN AND PRE-RAPHAELITISM IN THE UNITED STATES

....
William John Hennessy, Mon
Brave, *1870. The picture, depicting
a young woman mourning a dead
lover, alludes to the Franco Prussian
War of 1870.*
....

𝒫re-Raphaelitism appears, at first sight, to be a quintessentially historical style dependent upon a well-rehearsed idea of the distant past. It nursed, at least at its inception, the notion that medieval society was ethically and spiritually far superior to the modern age. This disposition was found not only in its paintings but also in the writings of Carlyle, Ruskin, Pugin and others. Pre-Raphaelite painting is, then, dependent upon a long cultural tradition and the belief that this tradition, once wholesome and worthy, underwent something of a fall from grace and was presently in a state of aesthetic corruption. Pre-Raphaelitism, of necessity, evolved in a cultural climate that could trace its origins back through not only centuries but millennia. It is perhaps surprising, therefore, to see a markedly original reworking of Ruskinian and Pre-Raphaelite ideas occurring in the United States, a nation which in the mid-19th century was less than 100 years old.

Ruskin's *Modern Painters* was first published in the United States in 1847. Some critics, like Franklin Dexter writing for the conservative *North American Review,* took exception to Ruskin's summary dismissal of the European academic tradition. Dexter restated the time-honoured belief that good painting was dependent upon the selective improvement of nature and that the most refined example of nature was best found not in the outside world but in great pictures. Other critics, like Margaret Fuller, were aware of the material preoccupations of many Americans and of the nation's limited cultural resources, and thought it prudent for the United States to maintain contact with a more mature culture. Many Americans, however, were of a more independent turn of mind, for *Modern Painters* appears to have been received with great enthusiasm and interest. Journals such as *The Massachusetts Quarterly Review* and *The Literary World* praised Ruskin for liberating art from the domination of the Old Masters, a sentiment echoed by many other contemporary critics.

Ruskin's supporters had found within *Modern Painters* a theoretical vein that was especially germane to their own cultural position. The very first Americans who had separated themselves from the colonial domination of Great Britain could, as revolutionary liberals, claim an affinity with the philosophers of the European Enlightenment. In the first part of the 19th century, however, ties between the United States and Europe were less well defined. Americans were psychologically dependent upon European culture

but, being thousands of miles away from their spiritual home, had little means of maintaining any real connection. There emerged around the middle of the century a debate that was to endure in some form for the next century, in which Americans were forced to choose between asserting a bond with Europe or hewing out a new and independent path of their own. It was in precisely this context that Ruskin's ideas (or, more accurately, a carefully selected part of his ideas) exerted so strong an appeal.

Modern Painters – if read selectively – upheld to artists the example of the ahistorical natural world in preference to the example of other art and provided American artists with an aesthetic standard remote from the values of European academies. As a consequence, Americans could paint and appreciate the immediate natural world around them, simultaneously forging a new painting style distinct from any European precedent. In fact, the critic Clarence Cook even suggested, somewhat imaginatively, that the cultural position of the United States was not dissimilar to that of medieval Europe or Classical Athens. The two societies had, he insisted, both fashioned an original and sophisticated culture without the assistance of a model. It followed, he maintained, that the possibilities for American art were boundless.

Ruskin's work was also to concur with American cultural interests on the spiritual as well as the nationalistic fronts. He had stressed the importance of naturalistic truth in art, and in *Modern Painters* had implied that this aesthetic mission had been accredited by Divine Creation itself. Americans, similarly, had long embraced the Low Church notion which maintained that God revealed himself to men and women not through priests and bishops but directly through the benign natural world. One Rev Samuel Osgood even saw landscape painting as a medium between Nature and Religion; he saw, furthermore, an affinity between the job of an artist and that of a minister, and had addressed the American Art Union in 1851 with a lecture tellingly entitled 'Art the Interpreter of Nature, Nature the Interpreter of God'. It was against this cultural backdrop that the unaffected poetry of William Wordsworth was widely admired, a disposi-

....
Frederick Edwin Church, Niagara
Falls, *1857. Church's celebrated
landscape was exhibited in London in
1857 and admired by John Ruskin.*
....

Arthur Hughes, Ophelia, *1852.*
One of several works by the artist
exhibited in the United States.

tion that was to lead to the rugged poetry of Walt Whitman some years later. It is, then, easy to appreciate why Ruskin found in the United States so attentive an audience – more attentive, he maintained, than his native readers – and why the critic, John Durand (son of the painter Asher B. Durand), credited Ruskin with doing more for disseminating a concern for painting in the United States than any other agency.

One influential springboard for the dissemination of Ruskinian theory in the United States was the publication of a journal entitled *The Crayon*. Produced by William James Stillman and Charles Eliot Norton, with John Durand as financial backer and William Michael Rossetti as foreign correspondent, *The Crayon* maintained a staunchly nationalistic editorial policy that upheld the native American landscape – assiduously recorded according to Ruskinian principles – as the prime concern for American painters. The journal had sniped at the venerable figure of Thomas Cole for including palm trees within his pictures (exotic flora, according to *The Crayon*, alien to native American landscape).

In addition, *The Crayon* had censured critic James Jackson Jarves for persistently asserting the importance of European painting for American artists. *The Crayon* steadfastly maintained that the inspiration of the natural world should remain unsullied by European interpretation. From its very inception in 1855, *The Crayon*, again following Ruskin's example, had appended to this preoccupation with the natural world some Divine intimation and had taken on an apostolic mission in which it would fight for a wholesome native culture against the distractions of a base and ungodly materialism. Writing in *The Crayon*, Stillman specified the bonds between God, Nature and Art. He stated:

> No man can revere Nature, save as he feels it to be only a form by which something higher than himself is manifested to him. . . .

Stillman continued:

> Reverence of Nature and consequent humility is, then, we assert, the first requisite of a religious art and in proportion as the artist grows in the perception of the spiritual meaning of Nature, and reads in her forms only Divine truth, he becomes more highly religious so that without possessing the full knowledge of truth which constitutes Christianity, his Art will still be religious in the degree of his light.

Those American critics and painters who were well disposed toward Ruskin invariably adapted his writings. It is rare, for instance, to find an American reference to the medievalism that was so crucial to the first and particularly the second volume of *Modern Painters* and thereafter in *The Seven Lamps of Architecture, The Stones of Venice* and *Academy Notes.* The carefully selective appreciation of Ruskin's writing is especially evident in the reception given to practical rather than theoretical examples of Ruskinian theory that came to the United States with the travelling exhibition of British art organized by Augustus A Ruxton in 1857.

Pre-Raphaelite painting – which *The Crayon* attributed to the sole influence of Ruskin – was represented in the exhibition and appeared to have attracted far greater attention than more conservative works by artists such as Frederick Leighton and Daniel Maclise. The exhibition opened in October at the National Academy of Design in New York. Conservative journals predictably praised anecdotal history paintings that were the stock in trade of middle-brow Victorian art, and, equally predictably, found Pre-Raphaelite submissions bewildering. Some found the fidelity to natural appearance within the works misplaced, while others thought the pictures 'rigid' and 'false'. While conservative American journalists were not renowned for their sensitivity, it is worth noting that the exhibition had a very mixed and in many respects an unrepresentative selection of Pre-Raphaelite pictures. From the very outset this study has referred to the enormous variety in the Brotherhood's output and the extent to which the circle constituted a coherent 'movement' for some five short years. In 1857, the United States glimpsed an insight into Pre-Raphaelitism while it was in a state of flux and while its members were going off on a number of contradictory tangents.

The exhibition included several seminal examples of Pre-Raphaelite painting such as Hunt's *The Light of the World* – dubbed by Rossetti as the movement's 'loftiest effort' – but also included some more demanding works. Ford Madox Brown submitted *Christ Washing Peter's Feet,* to which Boston's press took great exception, and Elizabeth Siddal was represented by a drawing entitled *Clerk Saunders,* to which *The New York Times* took an equal dislike. Such examples – given their complexity and rather idiosyncratic position within Pre-Raphaelitism as a whole – clearly placed considerable demands upon a new audience and while they may make sense in the context of Pre-Raphaelitism they provide a poor entry into the style for the uninitiated. It is also significant that two of the

three founder-members of the British circle, Millais and Rossetti, were not represented at the exhibition; the former could not coax his buyers to part with any pictures and Rossetti exhibited few pictures throughout the 1850s. Nonetheless Pre-Raphaelitism received some informed criticism, notably from Stillman and *The Crayon,* although this only occurred, on the whole, within the context of a very selective reading of Ruskin in which his historicism was replaced by God and Nature.

Stillman, writing in *The Crayon,* thought English Pre-Raphaelitism generally in keeping with American sensibilities but bemoaned the absence of landscape painting, commenting to W M Rossetti that that genre was far more appealing to American audiences than any of the Brotherhood's historical preoccupations. As a consequence, it was painters such as John Brett and John William Inchbold who received the most applause from both *The Crayon* and from less well-informed journals; when other Pre-Raphaelites won praise it was, in the main, for works in a similar genre. Brown's *Christ Washing Peter's Feet* may have been too demanding, but his *English Autumn Afternoon – London Outskirts* clearly appealed to American sensibilities.

This marked disposition toward landscape also served to elevate other, now largely forgotten, painters. Stillman enthused about the works of painters such as William Davis, Thomas Sutcliffe, WS Rose and WT Bolton, all of whom had confined themselves to modest but faithful accounts of the British landscape. In England, landscape painting accounted for only one among many divergent Pre-Raphaelite interests. In the United States, the arcane mysteries of symbolism or medieval history that had so engrossed British painters meant little; for the American audience, landscape exemplified Pre-Raphaelitism at its most articulate. It is hardly surprising, then, to discover that when, in 1863, American painters constituted their own fraternity along the lines of the English Brotherhood they were almost exclusively concerned with that one genre.

In January 1863 a group of artists and amateurs centred around the studio of the painter, Thomas Charles Farrer (1839–91), a one-time student of Ruskin at the Working Men's College in London, founded The Association for the Advancement of Truth in Art, a fraternity directly inspired by the example of the Pre-Raphaelite Brotherhood in England. Like the English Pre-Raphaelites, the majority of the members of the Association had also been with an academy, in this instance New York's National Academy of Design, and appear also to have been inspired by a similar spirit of secession.

American academies were less well-established and had less authority than their equivalents in Europe, although the Pennsylvania Academy of Fine Arts in Philadelphia, established in 1805, and New York's National Academy, founded in 1823, had, through a network of academicians, full teaching programmes and annual exhibitions, exercised strong nationwide influence. They had tended to support formal history painting executed in a picturesque manner – a style which had been commonplace in England in the first half of the 19th century. In an almost millennial summary of the annual exhibition of 1863, the Association dismissed the efforts of the National Academy, and confidently looked forward to the radical new initiatives of young American painters.

The Association for the Advancement of Truth in Art evolved out of a series of informal meetings among artists, critics and amateurs. These meetings gradually expanded to include the painters John William Hill (1812–79) and his son John Henry (1839–1922), William Trost Richards (1833–1905), Charles Herbert Moore (1840–1930), Henry Roderick Newman (1843–1917), and the influential art critic, Clarence Cook . On 27 January 1863 one such gathering attempted to establish some common purpose among its members and to clarify an artistic policy.

The nascent Association, which was infinitely better organized and more clear-sighted than its English counterpart, drafted a series of articles and elected a committee. JW Hill emerged as president of the Association and Clarence Cook was elected vice-president. Two other appointments, that of treasurer and secretary, were made and occupied, respectively, by Peter B Wight, an architect, and Clarence King, a geologist.

In addition to the reform of painting, the Association had also addressed itself to the reform of architecture and, again following Ruskin's example, upheld the Gothic idiom in preference to the Greek Revival style that had dominated building in the United States since the beginning of the 19th century. It is interesting, however, to see that so assiduous was the Association's interest in the scientific understanding of the natural landscape that it could also accommodate within its governing body the discipline of geology.

Ford Madox Brown, Christ
Washing Peter's Feet, 1851–1856.
A watercolour study of Brown's oil
painting was exhibited in Boston with
his King Lear and Cordelia of
1848–1849.

*Thomas Charles Farrer, Portrait of
Clarence Cook, c. 1861, pencil on
paper.*

The aims of the Association were, in fact, not dissimilar to those contained in *The Crayon*. It sought to sever all links with artistic tradition and to fashion a native American idiom according to the naturalistic standards upheld by Ruskin and the Pre-Raphaelites. A confident and independent American style would be afforded, the Association insisted, by a programme of art education, exhibitions and public instruction in both the applied and the fine arts. These objectives were set out in detail in the Association's journal, *The New Path*, first published in May 1863. The opening statement of the title page of the first issue, written by Cook, stated: 'The future of Art in America is not without hope . . . . The artists are nearly all young men; they are not hampered by too many traditions, and they enjoy the almost inestimable advantage of having no past, no masters and no schools.' Moreover, America's painters had the advantage, Cook insisted, of working for an uneducated public unburdened with the artistic prejudices that clouded the vision of European spectators.

The United States had, the journal noted, also begun to attain a mature culture of its own. *The New Path* conceded that an attachment to European culture had been necessary in the past. Now, however, it could start afresh and to this end the Association blithely wrote off the efforts of the previous generation. An article in the second edition of *The New Path* argued that academic art was of value only in that it provided an example to be avoided by others. At times the editorial tone of the journal rose from one of stridency to outright aggression. It was the Association's function, stated an article published in January 1864, to challenge academic complacency at all costs; its very purpose was to destroy undeserved reputations, and to promote discord and dissatisfaction among both artists and their public.

It is interesting to compare the tenor of American Pre-Raphaelitism with that of its English counterpart. Both organizations had sought artistic reform. The Pre-Raphaelite Brotherhood, however, had used stealth. It was a covert organization and might have remained so but for Rossetti's indiscretion. Its existence was marked only by the insignia secreted on some of its pictures and in some instances even this was omitted for fear of unfavourable critical attention. The Association, in contrast, made a full-scale assault on the academic establishment. It openly challenged conservative taste, upholding one standard of painting – that of literal truth – and proudly proclaiming 'we will not budge from the stand we have taken'.

Ruskin was a constant point of reference for the artists and writers connected with the Association, and several volumes of *The New Path* carried a published letter of support from the critic. Ruskin, however, was again used selectively by artists and critics who focused primarily on his call for fidelity to nature. The architect and critic, Russell Sturgis, contributing to *The New Path* in 1864, extended this aspect of Ruskinian theory dramatically and demanded that pictures be painted and judged according to the rigour of scientific standards; he insisted that a knowledge of the natural sciences of geology, botany and anatomy were essential to the task. Some critics connected with the Association were less demanding than Sturgis. Many had followed Ruskin's belief that mimesis alone was not enough and painting should be invested with some intellectual content, thus affording it some grand philosophical purpose. They were, however, unanimous in the belief that painstaking naturalism was the prime point of departure for sound painting and nothing of value could be achieved without it.

The United States had yet to produce a painter of, say, Turner's genius, although by addressing themselves to the diligent study of the natural world, American painters had taken, they believed, the only direction that could yield any comparable divided. It is symptomatic of *The New Path*'s asceticism that the course taken by the Association was a testing one. The joy of labour, according to Ruskin, is an important predicate for worthy art. His American interpreters, however, overlooked this aspect of his work and referred instead to the unflinching commitment required on the part of the artist. The highly finished technique advocated by *The New Path* was very labour-intensive and demanded astounding powers of concentration. In addition, their pictures had, of necessity, to be completed in the open air, often in inclement weather. The finished work, having taken so long to produce, would inevitably yield a poor financial return.

The pictures produced by the American Pre-Raphaelites fall into very distinctive categories quite separate from the work of their English counterparts. Few of the artists connected with the Association, for example, worked from the human figure. Instead they concentrated on either extensive landscapes or intensive nature studies, showing minutely detailed concentrations of flower, fruit and occasionally animal life.

....
ABOVE Thomas Charles Farrer,
Practicing her Lesson, *1859.*
....

....
RIGHT Thomas Charles Farrer,
Gone! Gone! *1860.*
....

The work of Thomas Charles Farrer is exceptional and his pictures are perhaps closest in aspiration to the work of the English Brotherhood.

Practicing her Lesson, drawn in 1859, shows a young woman at a piano with her back to the audience and her face reflected in an elaborate mirror. The drawing is made with meticulous and indiscriminate attention to detail. The woman's face, the most conspicuous part of the drawing, and the ornately patterned carpet and ball gown are given the same degree of finish. The drawing is reminiscent of Hunt's *Awakening Conscience,* although the principal difference between the two is that Farrer's work has no moral to impart. Hunt had painted his picture as a pendent to *The Light of the World;* it showed a fallen woman at her moment of spiritual redemption and was crammed with symbols – the bird, the song sheets, the cat and the lost glove – that alluded to her fate. Farrer's picture simply shows a well-to-do young woman, including no symbolism and implying no moral whatsoever.

Gone! Gone!, painted in 1860 and exhibited at the National Academy of Design the following year, is a closer approximation of English Pre-Raphaelitism; the artist has even acknowledged the lineage of the picture by inserting an engraving of Millais' *A Huguenot on St Bartholomew's Day* on the wall on the right-hand side of the painting. Millais and his comrades frequently used the theme of star-crossed lovers although in most instances the reason for their fate is specified through some historical or literary

Thomas Charles Farrer, Mount Tom, *1865.*

reference. Farrer offers no such explanation for his subject's distress save for the picture's title and the inclusion of an inscription on the frame from the Gospel of Matthew, Chapter 11 – 'Come unto me, all ye that labor and are heavy laden, and I will give you rest. Take my yoke upon you and learn of me; for I am meek and lowly in heart; and ye shall find rest unto your souls'.

Farrer's contribution to American Pre-Raphaelitism is somewhat atypical in that the majority of his contemporaries – following the advice of Ruskin and Cook – confined themselves to pictures of the immediate material (that is, natural) world. The work of John Henry Hill serves as a typical example. The younger Hill's *A Study of Trap Rock* of 1863, subtitled *Buttermilk Falls,* shows an outcrop of trap rock surrounded by dense vegetation; it was executed on location in the countryside of New Jersey. Other than the fact that Hill is bearing witness to Divine Creation – and here it is important to remember that geology would have had very different implications before the advent of scientific notions of history – the picture has no moral content.

This sense of materialism also characterizes the works of many of Hill's contemporaries, including his father, John William Hill, Moore, Richards and, in some instances, Farrer. Farrer's *A Buckwheat Field on Thomas Cole's Farm* (1863) and *Mount Tom* (1865) depict two extensive New England vistas rather than microscopic studies of nature, although in both instances the pictures are executed with the same unflinching attention to detail. Although Farrer painted *A Buckwheat Field* on a small canvas only 11¾ by 25in (29.8 × 64cm), he plotted his vista across the Hudson River from the Catskills with astonishing care.

Precisely the same principles used in the painting of landscape were applied to representations of still life. It was common for still-life paintings to be placed in a context showing fruit or flowers in a domestic setting.

....
John William Hill, Bird's Nest and
Dogroses, *1867.*
....

The Association's artists, however, redrafted this well-established, 17th-century tradition and located their studies of flowers or plants in their natural settings, often animating the scene with some remnant of animal life in the form of an egg or carcass of a bird. The paintings can in some respects be classified not as still-lifes but as landscapes with a remarkably restricted field of view and in this regard Ruskin was of the opinion that the principles underlying the world at large could also be found within the structure of individual specimens of rocks or plant life.

John William Hill's study of a bird's nest and dog roses made in 1867 is typical of its genre. The picture, executed in watercolour on a small scale, focuses attention on a fragment of a hedge as if the spectator were inches away from the object. Hills, Richards, Moore and Hunt each produced a number of equally detailed studies of this type, often amending traditional watercolour techniques to heighten a sense of naturalism. The genre is, in some respects, an invention peculiar to the Association, the practice evolving directly out of American Pre-Raphaelitism's materialist dogma.

The achievements of the Association for the Advancement of Truth in Art, despite the production of some breathtakingly realistic pictures, were somewhat limited. The Association's dependence upon dogma had restricted artists to the confines of landscape and

William Trost Richards, On the
Coast of New Jersey, 1883.

still-life that could only trade in the currency of the immediate, visible world. The psychological insights, sexual frustrations, and political and social dreams that had animated English Pre-Raphaelitism could not be admitted readily into the oeuvre of its American counterpart for the simple reason that these concerns were largely immaterial. Furthermore, the Association's ambitious attempts to reform the art world at large had patently failed. In 1865, less than three years after its inception, The New Path published its last edition. The Association itself, now independent of the journal, rapidly lost momentum, although some of its members continued to paint in the same style.

Despite the Association's limited achievements, some of the principles it held dear continued to play an important role in American cultural life. Ruskin, for example, had a profound effect on the arts in the United States, his example inspiring several generations of architects and designers, among them Gustav Stickley, Louis H Sullivan and Frank Lloyd Wright. The search for a style of painting that was free from the influence of Europe continued to preoccupy later American painters and finally found form in the work of the Abstract Expressionist school. Thereafter the problem was resolved. American painting achieved something of an apotheosis shortly after World War II and, free from the influence of Europe, it switched roles and started to dominate the fine arts on the other side of the Atlantic.

John William Hill, Peach
Blossoms, *1874, watercolour on
paper.*

John William Hill, Apple
Blossoms, *1874.*

CHAPTER SIX

THE

AESTHETIC MOVEMENT

THE FINAL YEARS OF PRE-RAPHAELITISM

....
*Dante Gabriel Rossetti, La
Ghirlandata, 1873. Painted at
Morris' home Kelmscott Manor. May
Morris modelled for the angels.*
....

re-Raphaelitism's demise was much less spectacular than its inception. The preceding chapters have plotted the increasing extent to which the interests of individual brethren varied, and this process was to continue during the last decades of the 19th century – until little trace of the original Brotherhood remained. The movement emerged out of the Romantic currents in European art, literature and thought. The same current of Romanticism, more virile and well articulated than the Pre-Raphaelite cause had ever been, finally absorbed most of its offspring.

The career of Sir Edward Coley Burne-Jones serves to demonstrate not only the thorough diversity of the Pre-Raphaelite oeuvre but also the degree to which it accorded with currents of Romantic art in England and abroad. Burne-Jones had initially worked with Morris's circle designing stained glass, tapestries and, later, book illustrations. Unlike Morris, he had continued to paint and, through the influence of G F

ABOVE Sir Edward Coley Burne-Jones, The Wise and Foolish Virgins, *1859.*

RIGHT Jacopo Tintoretto, The Annunciation.

Watts and Ruskin, evolved a distinctive style quite independent from that of his colleagues. Burne-Jones's style is far from the amalgam of archaism and naturalism found in early examples of Pre-Raphaelite painting. His pictures of the late 1860s and early 1870s are finely wrought, highly formalized figure studies variously reminiscent of the works of Giorgione, Botticelli and Michelangelo – and quite unlike the Quattrocento painting that had been so revered by many of his colleagues.

Burne-Jones's style had been formed, in part, through Ruskin's influence, although it is important to recognize that the critic's later concerns were quite different to those expounded in his earlier writings. Ruskin had undergone something of a change of heart around 1858 when he was, in his own words, 'unconverted' from the Evangelical doctrine to which he had hitherto subscribed. This loss of spiritual faith had prompted a profound revision of his aesthetic ideas and, by extension, Ruskin took an abrupt exception to medieval art. Instead he extolled an agnostic humanism and upheld the examples of Classical Greek art and Venetian painting, maintaining that a quintessential creative bond could be found between the apostolic examples of Phidias, Orcagna, Giotto, Titian and Tintoretto. Later Ruskin was to refer, somewhat disconcertingly, to idealized 'constants' within painting: invariably beautiful subjects in a 'state of perfect repose', where the formal quality of the work far outweighed any moral import. Ruskin had, in fact, moved perilously close to an approach that had been vilified universally by earlier Pre-Raphaelites, that is, the pagan formalism of the High Renaissance.

Burne-Jones's *The Wise and Foolish Virgins*, a pen and ink drawing of 1859, contains evidence of the influence of Ruskin's revised position. Part of the composition – the organization of figures on the left-hand part of the background – is reminiscent of a device used by Rossetti in *Mary Magdalene at the House of Simon the Pharisee*, although the drawing marks a significant swing away from what Ruskin now considered the trite medievalism that preoccupied Rossetti's circle. It is, for instance, significant that Burne-Jones has selected a biblical theme but has depicted the figures strung out through the composition in the manner of a Classical frieze. Burne-Jones frequently used a repertoire of either Christian, Classical or medieval subject matter without great discrimination. His classicism was to mature over the next decade and find form in works such as *Le Chant d'Amour*, begun in 1868 and completed over a period of nine years. The painting, inspired by an old Breton round, shows two women playing an organ before a young knight against a backdrop of medieval archi-

....
Sir Edward Coley Burne-Jones, The Golden Stairs, *1876-1880. First exhibited at the Grosvenor Gallery in 1880.*
....

....
L E F T *Aubrey Beardsley,* Messalina Returning Home.
....

tecture. Burne-Jones chose medieval subject matter, although the style in which *Le Chant d'Amour* was executed is extremely refined: the figures are idealized and have an ethereal, otherworldly quality. In most of these later works, an often ill-defined theme merely provides an excuse for a highly wrought arrangement of beautiful but rather introspective and morose young men and women, and the pictures impart a mood or sentiment rather than a particular moral or tale.

These characteristics are evident in the vast majority of Burne-Jones's paintings. In *The Golden Stairs,* painted between 1876 and 1880, 15 anonymous young women holding a variety of musical instruments descend a curved stone staircase. The picture has no overt content or allegorical message, a fact which mystified contemporary spectators weaned on the didacticism of most Victorian painters. Its anodyne subject aside, the artist has, however, focused attention on the picture's lyrical form, namely the flowing gestures and drapery of the classically inspired figures who swirl down the winding stairs.

The Wheel of Fortune and *Perseus Slaying the Sea Serpent,* both of which were begun in 1875, have readily identifiable subjects, although the pictures are party to the same dreamlike atmosphere as *The Golden Stairs,* in which even raging serpents can only raise a melancholy disinterest from their prey. In virtually every instance the subject of Burne-Jones's works are constrained within the same emotion which, in turn, finds its form in a series of beautiful coloured and linear affectations.

Form – the visible stuff from which a picture is composed, rather than its story or content – has been a long-standing preoccupation with 20th-century artists. For artists of the 19th century, the interest in the poetic quality of abstract forms was, in fact, a new departure in aesthetics. Sometime around the late 1870s, the Gothic style, with its wealth of historical and moral connotations, began to be upstaged in favour of a more amoral and abstracted attitude to art and architecture. The notion that art might exist for its own sake, independent of some moral purpose, had initially been imported from France. The poet Théophile Gautier was among the first to distinguish and separate artistic and ethical values. This notion had in turn been restated by critics such as Baudelaire, imported into England by Algernon Swinburne, and endorsed first by Walter Pater and later by his pupil, Oscar Wilde.

Advocacy of this amoral alternative to Victorian sentiment was popularly known as 'Aestheticism'. British Aesthetes, like their European counterparts, held the value of aesthetic sensation irrespective of the morality of its cuase; the disposition found an extreme form, for example, in the exploration into uncharted realms of sexual excess in the poetry of Swinburne and the designs of Aubrey Beardsley. Pater's contribution was more circumspect but no less radical in tone. He had argued in *The Renaissance,* published in 1873, that beauty was a largely subjective phenomenon, that it was indicative of the sensibility of the connoisseur and could, as a consequence, be found outside the established confines of art and literature.

George du Maurier satirized many of these pretentions in his cartoons for *Punch* in the early 1880s, in which his fictitious Aesthetes of Maudle, Postlethwaite and the Cimabue Browns regularly abandon themselves to the abstract formal contemplation of lilies, sunflowers, teapots and robust young country lads. The character of Maudle – a thinly disguised parody of Oscar Wilde – made one such appearance in *Punch* in February 1881: Maudle recognizes the consummate loveliness of one Mrs Brown's son. Mrs Brown, a philistine from the country, explains that her nice, manly boy intends to be an artist. 'Why,' Maudle demands, 'should he be anything? Why not let him remain for ever content to exist beautifully.' Du Maurier's view of Aestheticism was a satirical one although it was not without some foundation.

Oscar Wilde maintained the superiority of the decorative arts in his essay, 'The Critic as Artist', published in 1891. 'Mere colour,' he stated, 'unspoiled by meaning, and unallied with definite form, can speak to the soul in a thousand different ways'. He similarly upheld the authority of form over content in poetical metre. He continued:

He [the poet] does not first conceive an idea, and then say to himself 'I will put my idea into a complex metre of fourteen lines' but realising the beauty of the sonnet-scheme, he conceives certain modes of music and methods of rhyme, and the mere form suggests what is to fill it and make it intellectually and emotionally complete.

....
RIGHT George Frederick Watts,
The Judgement of Paris.
....

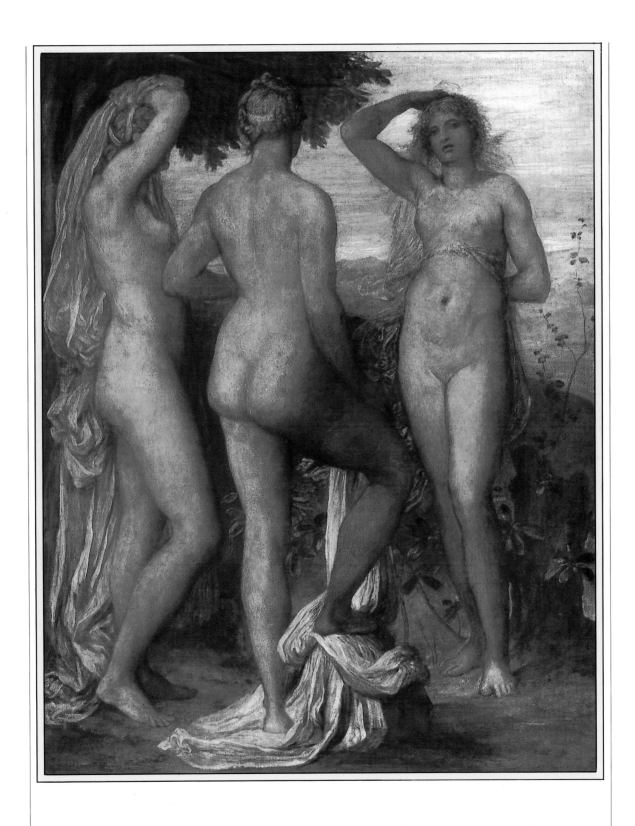

Pater, Wilde's mentor, similarly paid great attention to the form of a work of art and referred to the 'mode of handling', the means whereby the subject was presented to the spectator. For most Victorian painters, the form of their pictures was largely uncontentious in that it corresponded more or less to what the public generally agreed to be natural appearance. Pater, however, suggested that the form of a work of art had an autonomy and was an end in itself; it was, to use the catch-phrase, 'Art for Art's Sake'.

At first sight these arguments, which have had a profound influence on 20th-century painting, far greater than the Ruskinian principles they progressively displaced, seem somewhat abstracted and difficult to grasp. It is useful to compare Pater's interest in the formal and abstract qualities of a painting with the form of music. Music can be enormously evocative, yet it rarely communicates to us in a literal sense; rather, it evokes some mood or feeling through a configuration of sounds that have no literal meaning in themselves. It is perhaps significant that many contemporary painters, Burne-Jones and Whistler among them, made this comparison themselves, with Whistler going so far as to title his pictures with musical terms, such as 'Nocturne' and 'Symphony'.

The venue associated with Aestheticism in the late 1870s and 1880s was London's Grosvenor Gallery, established in 1877 under the direction of Sir Coutts Lindsay. Although Sir Coutts had no express intention of challenging the hegemony of the Royal Academy, the new establishment quickly became associated with more progressive trends in painting. Exhibition at the Grosvenor Gallery was by invitation rather than submission, and those invited to exhibit included James Tissot, Albert Moore, GF Watts, Richard Doyle, Giovanni Costa and George Howard. But the gallery's fame was primarily dependent upon its two most famous sons, Whistler and Burne-Jones. It was here that Whistler had exhibited the picture that prompted Ruskin's ire, the famous *Nocturne in Black and Gold*.

The dispute between Ruskin and Whistler is an interesting one, for it brings into sharp relief the two attitudes toward art abroad in late 19th-century England – the one mimetic and naturalistic, the other

imaginative and contingent upon the autonomy of the artist.

At the opening of the Grosvenor Gallery on May Day 1877, Whistler had exhibited a study of fireworks exploding in the night sky over the Italian town of Cremona. The picture was an exploratory one and, although a landscape, there were a few figurative references within the composition. Ruskin found it especially testing and accused its author of 'wilful imposture' and of 'flinging a paint pot in the face of the public'. Whistler sued Ruskin and a court case followed, in which the former won a Pyrrhic victory; he was awarded damages of one farthing although he was financially ruined by the legal costs.

The case centred upon the issue of finish. WP Frith saw no visible merit in the work and Burne-Jones, a reluctant witness on behalf of Ruskin, admitted that the picture was bewildering and had the qualities more often associated with a sketch. William Michael Rossetti and Albert Moore defended Whistler's painting, although a reading of the transcript of the trial shows that the Victorian legal establishment had little sympathy for the Aesthetic cause. Ruskin's vitriolic outburst was ungentlemanly, although the legal redress received by Whistler put the court's sympathies into some context.

Burne-Jones grudgingly defended Ruskin because of the support he had once received from his old friend, yet he could, in fact, have been a witness for Whistler's defence. Burne-Jones's formalism, his interest in an ethereal, dreamlike beauty and his refined feeling, inspired by often ill-defined or anonymous subject matter, was now light years away from the hard-nosed naturalism of his Pre-Raphaelite colleagues. Henry James's enthusiastic appraisal of Burne-Jones's painting as an art of 'reflection' and 'intellectual luxury', in a style inspired not by accidental reality but by an ornamental reflection on nature, is quite appropriate and shows the extent to which the artist had stepped outside the Pre-Raphaelite arena and into a current of Aestheticism.

Although Rossetti's influence on Burne-Jones began to wane as early as the mid-1860s, their respective pictures appear to be motivated by a similar spirit of mystique and melancholy (exacerbated in Rossetti's case by the death of Elizabeth Siddal). Among the most poignant of Rossetti's pictures of this period is *Beata Beatrix*, a devotional picture of Dante's sweetheart made in memory of his wife after her suicide in 1862. The picture shows Lizzie or Beatrice – the two

A B O V E Dante Gabriel Rossetti, The Blessed Damozel, *1871–1879. The predella shows an earth-bound figure looking up to his recently departed lover.*

L E F T Dante Gabriel Rossetti, The Bower Meadow, *1871–1872.*

are interchangeable in much of Rossetti's work – against the backdrop of Trecento Florence, with the twin figures of Dante and Love in the background. Beside Beatrice, her eyes closed and her head cast upward as if in an ecstatic trance, is a sundial marking nine o'clock – the hour Dante associated with Beatrice's death – and into her lap a dove casts a white poppy, the symbol of death. The ethereal quality of the picture is much enhanced by a hazy, soft-focus effect, a technique that had been used in the popular Victorian photographs of Julia Margaret Cameron.

The remainder of Rossetti's career was almost exclusively devoted to allegorical images of women, many in the form of devotional portraits. They include pictures such as *Regina Cordium*, *Monna Vanna* and *The Beloved*, all of which were painted around 1866. Rossetti's paintings of this period invariably paid far greater attention to abstract sentiment than to any story-line and, like Burne-Jones, he undertook several pictures with no overt subject matter whatsoever. *The Bower Meadow*, painted in 1872, and *La Ghirlandata*, made in the following year, were bought by FR Leyland, and both contain images of languid women playing musical instruments. They are devoid of any mythical or allegorical association, save perhaps for the sexual symbolism connected with the rose and honeysuckle.

Rossetti fell into a gradual process of decline after the death of his wife, terminating in his own death in 1882 at the age of 54. He depended on increasingly large doses of chloral hydrate and whiskey to cure chronic insomnia, and in 1872, after a poor critical review of a folio of his poetry, made an attempt on his life using laudanum, the same medium fatally administered used by his wife 10 years earlier. It was during the late 1860s that he began something approximating an affair with Jane Morris, who had become increasingly estranged from her husband. Jane and Rossetti spent considerable stretches of time together at Kelsmcott Manor in Oxfordshire (jointly rented by Morris and Rossetti), and the affair engendered a number of deeply contemplative and reverential studies of Jane in the guise of literary figures. These include Mariana from *Measure for Measure*; La Pia de' Tolomei from Dante's *Divine Comedy* and Proserpine, all three of whom had fates as unhappy or constrained lovers that closely reflected Jane's own relationship with Rossetti.

Rossetti, like his one-time protegé Burne-Jones, had also moved outside the established limits of Pre-

ABOVE Dante Gabriel Rossetti, Proserpine, *1874. First exhibited in Manchester, 1878.*

ABOVE RIGHT Ford Madox Brown, The Finding of Don Juan by Haidee, *1878. The subject is taken from Byron's* Don Juan, *Canto II, verses 110–112.*

Raphaelitism. Yet, unlike Burne-Jones, his painting had not been tempered with a contemplative asexuality. His painted and written portraits of Jane and other 'stunners' are riddled with a vivid physical and sensual appreciation of his subjects, warded off only by guilt and convention. Both Rossetti and Burne-Jones were of some importance to the unfolding literary and artistic interests of England and France in the late 19th century, and it was left to figures such as Swinburne and Wilde in England and the Symbolist and Decadent movements on the Continent to consummate the bond between art and sex had been divided by the vestigial code of Pre-Raphaelite chivalry.

The cult of Aestheticism, of which Rossetti and Burne-Jones were a part, inspired other members of the Pre-Raphaelite circle. Ford Madox Brown, for example, betrayed in his later works an interest in a linear, stylized design influenced by the cult. *The En-*

tombment (1868), originally intended as a cartoon for a church window, and *The Finding of Don Juan by Haidee* (1878) are formal and lyrical in design and quite unlike his earlier works. The majority of the younger generation of acolytes who remained were also, to varying degrees, affected by the cult of Aestheticism. The painter and illustrator, Simeon Solomon, the painter and poet, William Bell Scott, and Spencer Stanhope had all, through a variety of media, betrayed marked affinities toward the sensualism of Rossetti's circle and the Symbolist movement at large, and it appeared that the very notion of Pre-Raphaelitism was, by the latter part of the century, generally connected not with verisimilitude and naturalism but with the often lurid currency of Aestheticism.

Only William Holman Hunt had the tenacity to continue to apply the principles that had motivated the Brotherhood at its inception. He had undertaken a series of less spectacular but no less consistent pictures,

....
Spencer Stanhope, Psyche and
Charon.
....

portraits of friends such as *Mrs Thomas Fairbairn and
her Children; The King of Hearts;* and the painting of
London Bridge at night during the celebration of the
marriage of the Prince and Princess of Wales. Hunt
was, however, to return to the amalgam of naturalism
and historical accuracy applied in earlier works for
another series of pictures planned or painted in the
Middle East. In 1865 Hunt married Fanny Waugh.
The two left for the Holy Land in August the following year. A cholera epidemic delayed the couple in
Florence, and Hunt used the time to begin a painting
on the theme of Lorenzo and Isabella, an appropriate
one to tackle, he believed, in light of his enforced stay
in Florence. The picture, showing Isabella mourning
over her lover's remains contained within the traditional pot of basil, was to assume a special poignancy
after Fanny's death toward the end of the same year
(the work was eventually completed in England). Two
years later, however, Hunt made yet another visit to
the Middle East, one of three between 1869 and 1876,
where he began, among other works, *The Shadow of
Death* and the two versions of *The Triumph of the
Innocents.*

The Shadow of Death repeats the tried and tested
formula of Christian zeal and archaeological truth
that formed the backbone of the Pre-Raphaelite oeuvre
several decades earlier. Begun on location in Jerusalem in 1870, the picture is consistent with a branch of
enquiry, developed in mid-19th-century France, which
treated the life of Christ as of historical rather than
theological interest. It shows an event that has no
direct reference to the Gospels nor, as Hunt proudly
proclaimed, any supernatural component whatsoever. In this respect, Hunt maintained, the painting
was quite unique. Christ is depicted as having completed a long day's work, his arms outstretched in
relaxation. The image of a labouring Saviour was an
important one for Hunt; the pamphlet that accompanied the picture at its exhibition at London's
Agnew's Gallery in 1873 explained that the work was
about the 'burdensomeness of toil and the relief at its
cessation', and that Hunt chose to show Christ in the
carpenter's shop as the paradigm of the dignified
labourer.

Consistent with the original principles of Pre-

....
ABOVE William Holman Hunt,
May Morning on Magdalen
Tower, *1890.*
....
LEFT William Holman Hunt, The
Lady of Shalott, *c. 1889–1892.*
....

....
Sir John Everett Millais, Autumn
Leaves, *1855–1856. First exhibited
at the Royal Academy, 1856.*
....

Sir John Everett Millais, The Blind
Girl, *1854–1856. First exhibited at
the Royal Academy, 1856.*

A B O V E Sir John Everett Millais,
Sir Isumbras at the Ford, *1857.*

....

R I G H T Sir John Everett Millais,
My First Sermon.

....

Raphaelitism, Christ's repose is anything but straightforward, for in his moment of rest at the end of a long day's work he assumes an eerie posture, that of crucifixion. Lest anyone miss the overt symbolism, Hunt casts Christ's shadow across a wooden rack of tools (instruments of the Passion in earlier Pre-Raphaelite works), thereby forming a chilling prefigurative image of the Crucifixion. The shadow cast on the wall of the workshop arrests the attention of Christ's mother, who kneels with her back to the spectator beside a chest containing the gifts of the Magi. Mary assumes, in fact, a posture more common to 15th-century scenes of the Annunciation, although in this instance the Archangel is exchanged for the vision of the cross and it is Christ's death rather than his birth that is announced. Scattered about the room are an array of symbolic objects: a red fillet – seen as a symbol of sin in *The Scapegoat* – is shown here as the crown of thorns; reeds at left represent the sceptre thrust into Christ's hand at the Crucifixion, and pomegranates – traditional symbols of the Passion – rest on the window sill. Contemporary critics were also able to discover further layers of symbolism: the arched window was seen as a nimbus, the star-shaped window had obvious connotations, and Mary's turn away from the viewer was imaginatively read as an anti-Catholic gesture.

Among the most conspicuous of Hunt's other biblical pictures of the period are the two versions of *The Triumph of the Innocents,* painted between 1876–87 and 1880–84, respectively. The pictures are among the most important in the last chapter of Hunt's career and use quite a different formula from earlier works. The two rework the traditional scene of the Flight into Egypt, although in these instances Hunt's characteristic verisimilitude is compromised by the inclusion of a vision of a cavalcade of Innocents, the first Christian martyrs. Hunt clarified his intentions in a written commentary, stating that the Innocents, who ride into the picture on the Waters of Life while displaying prefigurative symbols of Christ's own fate, had no corporeal substance and were part of a vision accorded to the Holy Family. Hunt's work, hitherto preoccupied with the material facts of the Gospels, now retreats into a profoundly idiosyncratic and unlovely flight of fancy.

The remainder of Hunt's career was less than prolific. Save for *May Morning on Magdalen Tower* (1888–91); *The Lady of Shalott* (1886–1905), and a copy of his much loved *The Light of the World,* which hangs in London's St Paul's Cathedral, Hunt clarified his

ambitions in print rather than paint. Testimony to his understanding of the aims of the Pre-Raphaelite circle and his seminal role within it, so he maintained, as its spiritual and intellectual leader, is his *Pre-Raphaelitism and the Pre-Raphaelite Brotherhood,* published five years before his September 1910 death.

Hunt's memoirs betray the belief that he considered himself the only faithful apostle of Pre-Raphaelitism, working against a tide of Aesthetic and Symbolist affectations that had touched his colleagues and their associates. John Everett Millais was a notable exception, for he was faithful neither to the original spirit of Pre-Raphaelitism nor to its romantic offshoot. Millais, the most conspicuously talented of all of the founder-members of the circle, soon lost the radical calling seen in earlier works. He had been profoundly unnerved by the harsh criticism initially received from the press in the early 1850s, and over the next decade or so he became increasingly timorous in his approach, progressively integrating himself into the artistic establishment. Dining with the Prince of Wales at a party held in the 1880s, Millais estimated that he had earned over £40,000 per year and could have increased the sum easily had he not taken so long a holiday. Social and financial success had, however, taken its toll on the quality of his work.

Millais continued to gain the critical approval of Ruskin with the exhibition of *The Rescue* in 1855, a picture celebrating the work of the London Fire Brigade, whose heroism, unlike that of the military, had remained unsung in painting. The melancholy *Autumn Leaves* and *The Blind Girl,* both shown at the Academy during 1856, were also well received, although the approval was remarkable when one considers that the artist had only recently absconded with Effie Gray Ruskin, the critic's wife, resulting in the embarrassing annulment of Effie's and Ruskin's marriage. *Autumn Leaves* has no clearly defined subject. It shows a group of children contemplative in mood standing around a pile of fallen leaves at dusk. The subject was partly inspired by the poetry of Tennyson and William Allingham and contains an obvious allusion to the transience of life and the imminence of death and decay. The child on the right of the picture stares

....
*R I G H T Sir John Everett Millais,
print made from* Cherry Ripe,
1879.
....

mournfully at the leaves and holds an apple (a symbol of autumn and of the Fall) in her right hand. An equally melancholy but less obscure note is struck in *The Blind Girl*. The piture is concerned with a contemporary preoccupation with vagrancy among the young and disabled; in this instance Millais has dramatically contrasted the blindness of the young girl (who appears within *Autumn Leaves)* with the ravishing beauty of the minutely detailed landscape that surrounds her.

Millais' exhibition of *Sir Isumbras at the Ford*, painted in 1857, marked a particularly violent fall from artistic grace as far as Ruskin was concerned. The picture shows two children clasped to the side of an aging knight crossing a ford on his steed. The subject has no particular literary or mythical source, although the picture was accompanied by a tortured pseudo-medieval poem by Thomas Taylor that sought to justify, among other things, the absurdly large black horse. Ruskin balked not only at the size of the mount but also at the slapdash and unrealistic manner in which colour had been applied to the landscape. The armour was also deemed poorly painted, in that it neither shined and reflected the light and colour around it nor looked appropriately dulled and battle-scarred. Millais' decline – which as far as Ruskin was concerned had now assumed catastrophic proportions – was marked by not only *Sir Isumbras* but also by another 'failure', *The Escape of the Heretic*, painted in the same year.

Millais' decline has become an accepted part of the Pre-Raphaelite annals, although his fall was far from total and he redeemed himself by a number of absorbing pictures. The melancholy study of two nuns digging in a graveyard, *The Vale of Rest* of 1858, serves as an example. It was painted on location in a cemetery in Scotland and refers to the eventual deaths of the two sisters and their final union with Christ (symbolized in the picture by two wedding rings in the form of a golden wreath). Millais has, somewhat chillingly,

also given the spectator some common purpose with the two nuns by siting their viewpoint as if the onlooker was standing at the bottom of the grave. The morbid mood of the painting is further endorsed by the declining light and the coffinlike cloud (which, according to Scottish lore, prefigures death) floating across the evening sky and, not least, by the gaze of the figure on the right, who sports a memento *mori* on her rosary.

Offset against some inconsistent work, the best of which clearly lacks the application and purpose of Millais' earlier painting, are a body of much less compulsive, often saccharine and commercial pictures. They include *My First Sermon*, painted in 1862–63; *Leisure Hours*, exhibited at the Royal Academy the following year; *Cherry Ripe* of 1879 (colour reproductions of which ran to well over half a million copies), and society portraits, such as *Hearts are Trumps*. The corpus also comprised other essential but hardly worthy components of the Pre-Raphaelite canon – works such as *The Boyhood of Raleigh* and *Soap Bubbles*, the apotheosis of Millais' singularly popular style. In many respects, it is ironic that Millais' later pictures endeared him to an ill-schooled and philistine public, one which, a generation or so earlier, recoiled at the Brotherhood's zealous attempts to reform British painting. Millais' reconciliation with the establishment was complete. He had been made a full Academician in 1860 and was awarded a baronetcy in 1885, the first British painter to be so honoured. In 1896 he became president of the bastion of the artistic establishment, the Royal Academy.

The anti-establishment banner of artistic reform that had once been carried by Millais and his colleagues – who had in fact constituted the first 'movement' within the history of modern painting – was now passed on. The most aggressive and artistic challenges to the bourgeois status quo occurred now not in philistine England but abroad, first and foremost in bohemian France.

....
L E F T Sir John Everett Millais,
Bubbles.
....

SELECT BIBLIOGRAPHY

The author wishes to acknowledge his debt to many sources and recommends the following select bibliography for further reading:

ADAMS, Steven, *The Arts and Crafts Movement* (London, 1987)

ANDREWS, Keith, *The Nazarenes* (Oxford, 1954)

ASLIN, Elizabeth, *The Aesthetic Movement: Prelude to Art Nouveau* (London, 1969)

BELL, Quentin, *A New and Noble School – The Pre-Raphaelites* (London, 1982)

EVANS, Joan, *John Ruskin* (London, 1954)

FERBER, Linda and GERDTS, William, *The New Path: Ruskin and the American Pre-Raphaelites* (Brooklyn, 1985)

GAUNT, William, *The Pre-Raphaelite Tragedy* (London, 1975)

GRIEVE, Alistair, *The Art of Dante Gabriel Rossetti* (London, 1975)

HENDERSON, Philip, *William Morris, His Life, Work and Friends* (London, 1967)

HILTON, Timothy, *The Pre-Raphaelites* (London, 1970)

HUNT, Diana Holman, *My Grandfather, His Wives and Loves* (London, 1969)

HUNT, John Dixon, *The Pre-Raphaelite Imagination, 1848–1900* (London, 1968)

HUNT, William Holman, *Pre-Raphaelitism and the Pre-Raphaelite Brotherhood* (London, 1905)

LANDOW, George P, *William Holman Hunt and Typological Symbolism* (New Haven, Conn., 1979)

LYNES, Russel, *The Art Makers* (New York, 1970)

ROSE, Andrea, *Pre-Raphaelite Portraits* (Oxford, 1981)

ROSSETTI, William Michael, *The PRB Journal* (Oxford, 1975)

SPALDING, Francis, *Magnificent Dreams: Burne-Jones and the Late Victorians* (London, 1978)

SPENCER, Robin, *The Aesthetic Movement* (London, 1972)

STEEGMAN, John, *Victorian Taste* (London, 1987)

STALEY, Alan, *The Pre-Raphaelite Landscape* (Oxford, 1973)

STEIN, Roger B, *Ruskin and Aesthetic Thought in America, 1840–1900* (Cambridge, Mass., 1967)

SURTEES, Virginia, *The Paintings and Drawings of Dante Gabriel Rossetti 1828–1882* (Oxford, 1971)

TATE GALLERY, *The Pre-Raphaelites* (London, 1984)

THOMPSON, Edward, *William Morris, Romantic to Revolutionary* (London, 1955)

WATKINSON, Ray, *Pre-Raphaelite Art and Design* (London, 1970)